Gregg Bordowitz

Sam Lewitt

Josephine Meckseper

Matt Mullican

AF271629

on

Hanne Darboven

2,) Iudex: 01, 10, -2X

3 K - 44 K / 42 No

1 + 1 + 0 + 1 - 3 ——— 42 No ——— 31 + 12 + 0 + 1 - 44

1 + 1 + 1 + 0 - 3 ——— 42 No ——— 31 + 12 + 1 + 0 - 44

3 K ————————————————→ 44 K

Gregg Bordowitz
Sam Lewitt
Josephine Meckseper
Matt Mullican

Artists on
Hanne Darboven

Edited by Stephen Hoban and Kelly Kivland
with Katherine Atkins

Artists on Artists Lecture Series
Dia Art Foundation

A publication of the Sackler Institute at Dia Art Foundation.

Support for *Artists on Hanne Darboven* has been provided by Konrad Fischer Galerie.

ISBN 978-0-944521-82-3

A version of "A Lecture on Hanne Darboven" by Matt Mullican was previously published in *The Order of Time and Things: The Home-Studio of Hanne Darboven* (Madrid: Museo Nacional Centro de Arte Reina Sofía, 2014).

Dia Art Foundation
535 West 22nd Street
New York, NY 10011
www.diaart.org

Distributed by
ARTBOOK | D.A.P.
75 Broad Street, Suite 630
New York, NY 10004
T: (212) 627-1999
F: (212) 627-9484
www.artbook.com

Book design: Laura Fields
Series editors: Stephen Hoban and Kelly Kivland
Text editors: Katherine Atkins and Stephen Hoban
Research assistance: Claire Dilworth
Proofreader: Nancy Moore Hulnick

Printed in Belgium by die Keure, nv

Library of Congress Cataloging-in-Publication Data
Names: Bordowitz, Gregg. | Lewitt, Sam, 1981- | Meckseper, Josephine, 1964- |
   Mullican, Matt, 1951- | Dia Art Foundation, issuing body.
Title: Artists on Hanne Darboven.
Description: New York : Dia Art Foundation, 2016. | Series: Artists on
   artists lecture series | Includes bibliographical references.
Identifiers: LCCN 2016045054 | ISBN 9780944521823 (pbk.)
Subjects: LCSH: Darboven, Hanne--Criticism and interpretation. | Darboven,
   Hanne. Kulturgeschichte 1880-1983.
Classification: LCC N6888.D37 A87 2016 | DDC 709.2--dc23
LC record available at https://lccn.loc.gov/2016045054

Frontispiece: Hanne Darboven, *Kulturgeschichte 1880–1983 (Cultural History 1880–1983)*, 1980–83. Detail: II/145

CONTENTS

PREFACE

Since 2001, Dia Art Foundation has presented the Artists on Artists Lecture Series in New York City. The series welcomes practicing artists to join the critical discussion on artists from Dia's history; the care and insight that our invited artists have brought to their informal lectures, talks, and performances have turned these presentations into memorable and cherished events. We have had the opportunity to learn as much about the practice of the artist speaking as we have had the chance to hear original perspectives into the work of artists long associated with Dia. Many of these lectures are now preserved for listening and viewing on Dia's website. The series, which is currently celebrating its fifteenth year, would not have been possible without the help of many generous funders. Over the history of the program our supporters have included Art for Art's Sake, Nancy Miller, the New York City Department of Cultural Affairs, Cindy and Howard Rachofsky, the Dr. Mortimer and Theresa Sackler Foundation, and the SEA Foundation. Thanks is also due to Konrad Fischer Galerie, which has supported the creation of this publication.

We are dedicating the inaugural volume of this new Artists on Artists publication series to Hanne Darboven, honoring the 2016–17 installation of *Kulturgeschichte 1880–1983* (*Cultural History 1880– 1983*, 1980–83) at Dia:Chelsea in New York City. We would like to thank the artists included here—Gregg Bordowitz, Sam Lewitt, Josephine Meckseper, and Matt Mullican—who have been generous with their time as we prepared their talks for publication. Florentine Gallwas and Nicole Krapat from the Hanne Darboven Foundation, Hamburg, embraced the idea of bringing these talks to a broader audience. The dedication of Dia's staff over the years has made the Artists on Artists Lecture Series a success. Former curator Lynne Cooke initiated the series, which is today ably run by associate curator Kelly Kivland with technical assistance from Max Tannone. Through the years the program has also benefited from the diligent efforts of Jeanne Dreskin, Patrick Heilman, Kristin Poor, and Yasmil Raymond. Katherine Atkins and Stephen Hoban edited the texts collected here, and Claire Dilworth tracked down many hard-to-find images. We are grateful to Laura Fields, whose thoughtful design captures both the intimacy and immediacy of these talks.

Dia looks forward to continuing this valuable lecture series and to publishing the artists' unique voices in subsequent collections.

Jessica Morgan
Director, Dia Art Foundation

INTRODUCTION

Initiated in May 2001, Dia Art Foundation's Artists on Artists Lecture Series is a public program focused on providing artists' perspectives on individual artists represented in Dia's collection, exhibitions, or programming. Each spring and fall, contemporary artists are invited to each speak on an artist of her or his choosing. The program intentionally values varied approaches of address from scholarly lectures to personal reflections and performances. The long-standing series has become a beloved program in New York City, where artists, students, writers, and cultural peers gather to discuss, ruminate, and even challenge well-known positions on various artists of the twentieth century. The longevity of the Artists on Artists Lecture Series is a testament to its being a platform where ideas—whether logical assertions or introspective nonlinear divergences—can be aired with assurance. Such openness allows an artist to both put herself or himself in relation to the work of another artist as well as reflect on her or his own practice.

Now in its fifteenth year, the Artists on Artists Lecture Series has featured over ninety voices. To mark the occasion of this seminal anniversary, Dia was compelled to begin a publication series that shares the lectures' legacy more widely in contemporary discourse.

This inaugural book focuses on Hanne Darboven, and is being released in connection with Dia's third presentation of Darboven's seminal and vast work, *Kulturgeschichte 1880–1983* (*Cultural History 1880–1983*, 1980–83). She was born in 1941 in Munich. The second of three daughters in an upper-middle-class family, Darboven was raised in a suburb of Hamburg. She studied piano and enjoyed science, practices which led her to a personal interest in accumulation, inscription, and repetition. Living in New York City from 1966 to 1968, she not only met great Conceptual thinkers of the time—including Sol LeWitt and Lucy Lippard—but also encountered political and social unrest that brought forth great similarities to her upbringing in postwar Germany. She then returned to her family's home, where she lived for the rest of her life.

The cultural influences leading up to and following the postwar era are continuous themes throughout Darboven's practice. This is evident in *Cultural History*, the epic floor-to-ceiling installation composed of thousands of pieces of printed matter and nineteen sculptural objects. The overwhelming mass of information presented would take days to parse and unravel. The rigorous yet rhythmic display of the installation calls out to the viewer to be read, to spend unrestricted time piecing together associations. Such an act is indicative of the artist's life practice. She dedicated her career to questions around language, memory, systems, time, and labor, which she engaged in varied forms, including musical notation, personal letters, large-scale installations, and abstract films.

Even upon her death, Darboven's pursuit of self-knowledge—by accumulating, by writing, by documenting, by displaying, by looking, by transcribing, by listing, by thinking—was never exhausted. This in many ways harks back to the premise of the Artists on Artists Lecture Series, which invites contemporary artists to take up questions that continue to surround an artist's work.

What follows are perspectives on Darboven from four artists who have presented in the series over the past ten years: Gregg Bordowitz (2016), Sam Lewitt (2014), Josephine Meckseper (2011), and Matt Mullican (2006). Each brings forth Darboven's ardor to allow the viewer a singular experience—to see what they see, to hear what they hear, to process how they process, and to associate as they associate.

Kelly Kivland
Associate Curator, Dia Art Foundation

Gregg Bordowitz
Timed Transcription

The following text is a lightly edited transcript of a talk delivered at Dia:Chelsea on Tuesday, February 2, 2016, starting at 6:30 pm.

00:07:10:04

BORDOWITZ: And this is going to be somewhat personal. I'm going to talk about Hanne Darboven's work largely, mostly *Kulturgeschichte 1880–1983* [*Cultural History 1880–1983*, 1980–83], but some of the early work too. And also I'm going to talk about Darboven in a way that I think is idiosyncratic, because her work—I realized by composing this presentation that my appreciation for Darboven is long and abiding. It's thirty years old. I'll talk about my first encounter with her work around thirty years ago and how I have remained interested and curious about her work since then. This most recent period of research made me realize a lot of things about historicization, which I'm going to talk about in a bit.

00:08:11:16

First, I want to start by reading some basic protocols for making art. The basic protocol for the creation of any work of art follows four considerations: What falls inside the frame? What falls outside the frame? Who stands beholding the work? What does the work of art itself present as a matter of composition? The work of art, when it is encountered, includes the present moment of the encounter, the past preceding the encounter, what occurs after the encounter, what is remembered of the encounter. The work of art and the viewer's engagement with art also includes the possibility that a work of art was never encountered; the

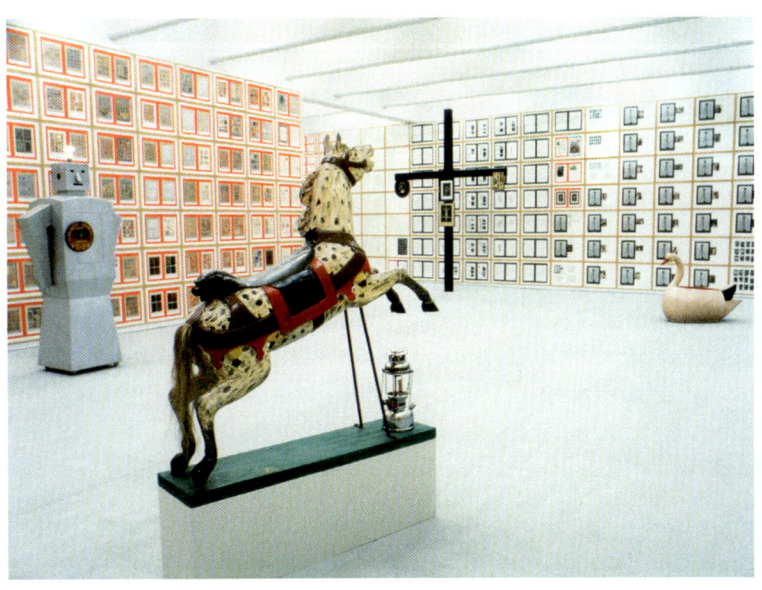

Cultural History 1880–1983, 1980–83. Dia Center for the Arts, New York, 1996–97

work was glimpsed, but forgotten; elements of the art object elude notice, while some features remain. Here, I am referring to multiple states of consciousness occupying the individual viewer, multiple viewers, the artist or creator of a particular artwork, alongside artists, both past, present, and future, real and imagined, all participants coinciding to bear upon this moment, this enactment, this now. How do we account for all the variables affecting creation?

00:09:52:00

I'm going to start by showing slides of *Cultural History*, which was acquired by Dia under the curatorship of Lynne Cooke and shown in the late nineties, 1996–97, I believe, and has not shown since then in New York but was just recently shown in Munich, at Haus der Kunst, where I had the good fortune of traveling to view the installation with my good friend Jason Simon. So I'm going to actually show you these slides I got from Dia. These are the installation shots of *Cultural History* that were taken during Dia's installation in the late nineties. I'll just read a little bit from the press release. I'm showing this because some of you may have seen it; some of you don't recall it; many of you may have not seen it.

00:10:58:08

[*Cultural History*] consists of 1,590 wall-mounted panels of uniform size and format and nineteen objects. It traces one hundred years of history, via a miscellany of images and texts that range from postcards to art reproductions, portraits of film stars, and the covers of weekly magazines. Many bear handwritten notes and quotations. Over the past thirty years, Darboven created a vast body of work based on time, as registered by history and by memory alike. Beginning with the date, whose numbers she manipulate[d] into a temporal and chronological system, Darboven has in

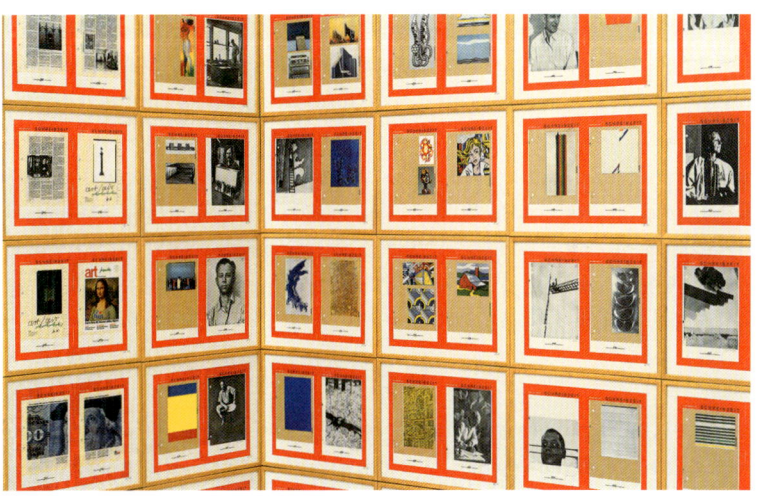

Cultural History 1880–1983. Dia Center for the Arts, 1996–97

[*Cultural History*] constructed an encompassing, encyclopedic archive that fuses public history and collective memory with personal experience.

That's from the press release that Dia issued at the time.

00:12:00:28

So as you can see, there are more than 1,500 panels of uniform size. And they are distributed according to specific parameters. The piece institutes itself. It's numbered in a serial fashion, so that it lays itself out on the walls. The curator can decide how far to go up on the wall. It's largely determined by architecture. In Munich, as you'll see, the panels went up higher than they did in the Dia installation, and the wall panels lay themselves out accordingly. The objects, the nineteen sculptural objects—and you see three of them here in this image; you're seeing them, right? [MAN: Yep] Yeah? And you're hearing me? You're hearing me okay? [VOICES: Yeah] Alright.

00:12:55:21

So here's more panels with more objects. That's a post or column that many of you will recognize. You often see these posts in European countries, where posters are pasted on them announcing cultural events. In the one in Munich, there're actually Hanne Darboven posters on that column. There are statuettes distributed throughout. There's this strange carnival horse that looks like it might be something off of a merry-go-round. And again, you can see the panels behind. I have some close-up details of the panels. Again, images, objects. There's a huge cross in the middle of the exhibition, with images appended. And I have close-ups of the images that are appended. There's a child's chair, there are more statuettes and a hanging crescent with a musical composition attached to it. More statuettes. This really bizarre wooden robot with a clock on its chest. These are all the Dia shots. Store mannequins with period—what looks like to be late seventies, early eighties—gym wear,

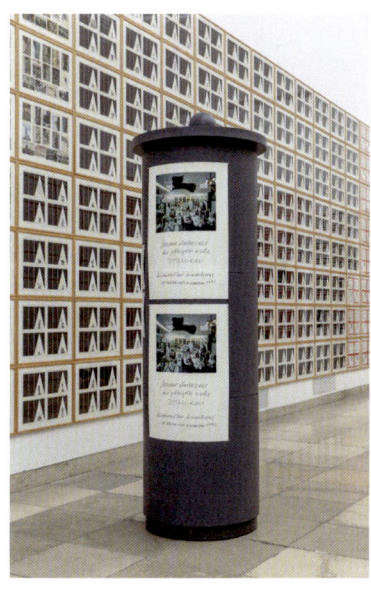
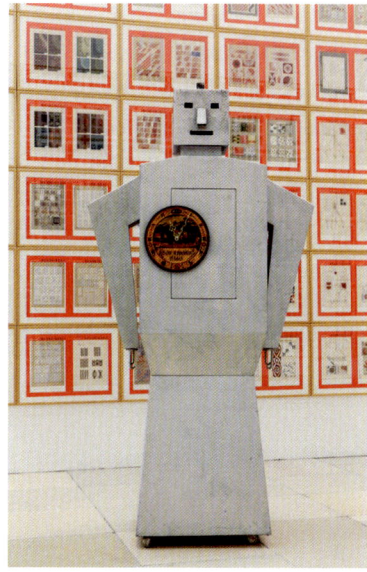
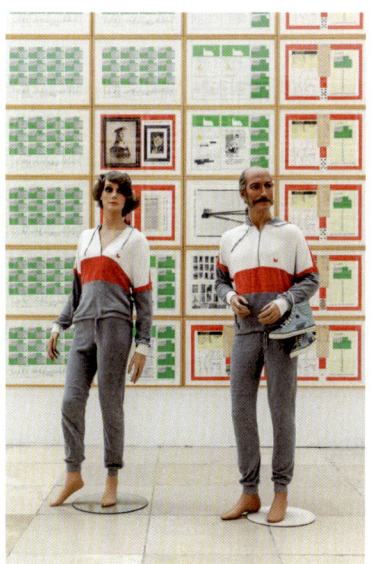
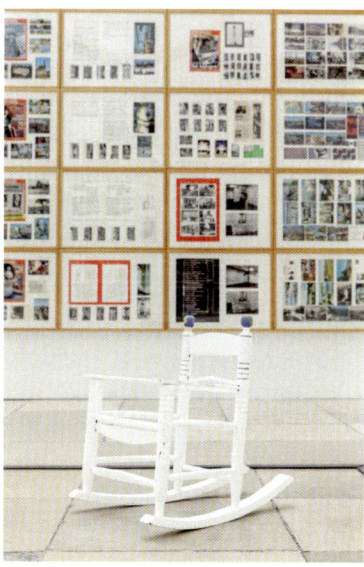

Cultural History 1880–1983. Haus der Kunst, Munich, 2015

sweat suits. These figures, which I have other images of, one is a doctor and one is a butcher. They're figures that would be outside of a shop or store. There's actually a stuffed animal sculpture, which I have another picture of.

00:14:48:23

This is what the panels look like. They're combinations of images, hand-writing with that—you could call it signature cursive writing that's associated with Darboven, this endless I or U. It's not a letter; I shouldn't even really say that. It's a mark that repeats and recurs throughout her work. Of course, that's an image of Rainer Werner Fassbinder and Hanna Schygulla. And then there's a postcard. The panels have pictures that are pasted on top of newspapers, and other elements—captions and quotes, quotations associated with the images or not associated with the images—fall under the images. Strange taxonomies that are—

00:15:47:23

This is almost like a poem, I think. And I'm going to talk a lot about poetry and the relationship of Darboven to poetry. Darboven was very interested in poetry, particularly Baudelaire, Heine, and Rilke. She did an entire piece based on [Rainer Maria] Rilke's *Book of Images*, which I'm not going to show, but I will discuss her relationship to poetry. Here you see that there are images that rhyme, images that are maybe culled from the same reservoir of material. The geography of some of the places is not the same. So it's hard to discern. There are overlapping taxonomies which are interrelated and relate to the surrounding panels. And you see a lot of repetitions within the surrounding panels of *Cultural History*. There's pictures of movie stars, Marlene Dietrich and Humphrey Bogart and Marilyn Monroe. There's also pictures of rock stars. Van Halen and Rush and Bruce Springsteen.

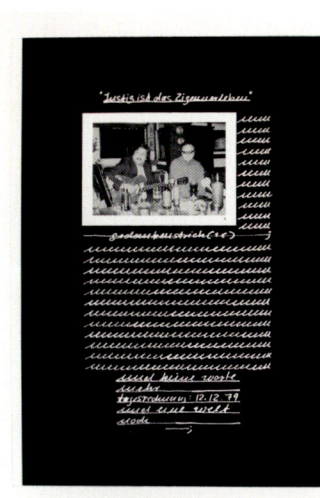

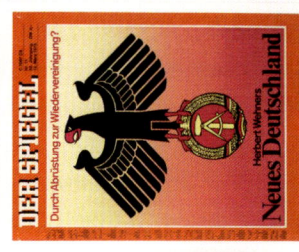

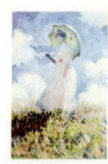

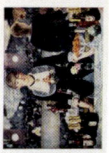

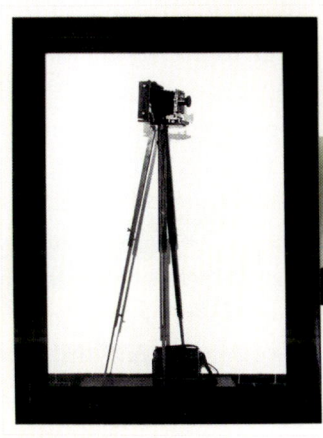

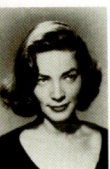

Cultural History 1880–1983. Detail: IV/179
Cultural History 1880–1983. Detail: III/199

00:16:53:23

This is not *Cultural History*; this is another piece that is based on four people who Darboven was interested in: Gertrude Stein, Virginia Woolf, Marie Curie, and Rosa Luxemburg. In the middle of this piece, there's a female mannequin figure that is armless. This is also the Haus der Kunst in Munich. Those are the statuettes, the same statuettes that were in Dia, but placed differently. I'm given to understand, even though I said that the piece institutes itself, that the curator of *Cultural History* has some latitude as to where to place the objects. It's not necessarily specified by Darboven where the objects should fall in relationship to the panels behind the objects.

00:18:01:12

Again, more pictures. This is from Haus der Kunst. Behind this statuette and this image of the sailor are images of doors, hundreds of images of doors, that were taken in New York City by Roy Colmer, who was a good friend of Darboven. This is the layout in the Haus der Kunst. You see the same elements from the Dia installation placed differently in Munich. Here's the robot. Here's a closer image of the robot. That swan, it's interesting to me; a child could fit into it. I think it's probably from some amusement park ride. Here are the figures of the butcher and the doctor. And a wooden sculpture. There's the crescent. The child's chair. There, you get a sense of how the panels operate behind the object in front. There's a huge section with two covers of *Der Spiegel* per each pane. And there's that image of the sweat suits. A stuffed animal–doll sculpture.

00:19:22:10

This is the cross in the middle of the exhibition. This is some folkloric image of children. There's a soldier, another image of Christ on the cross, another image of Christ. A nineteenth-century figure. A bell or

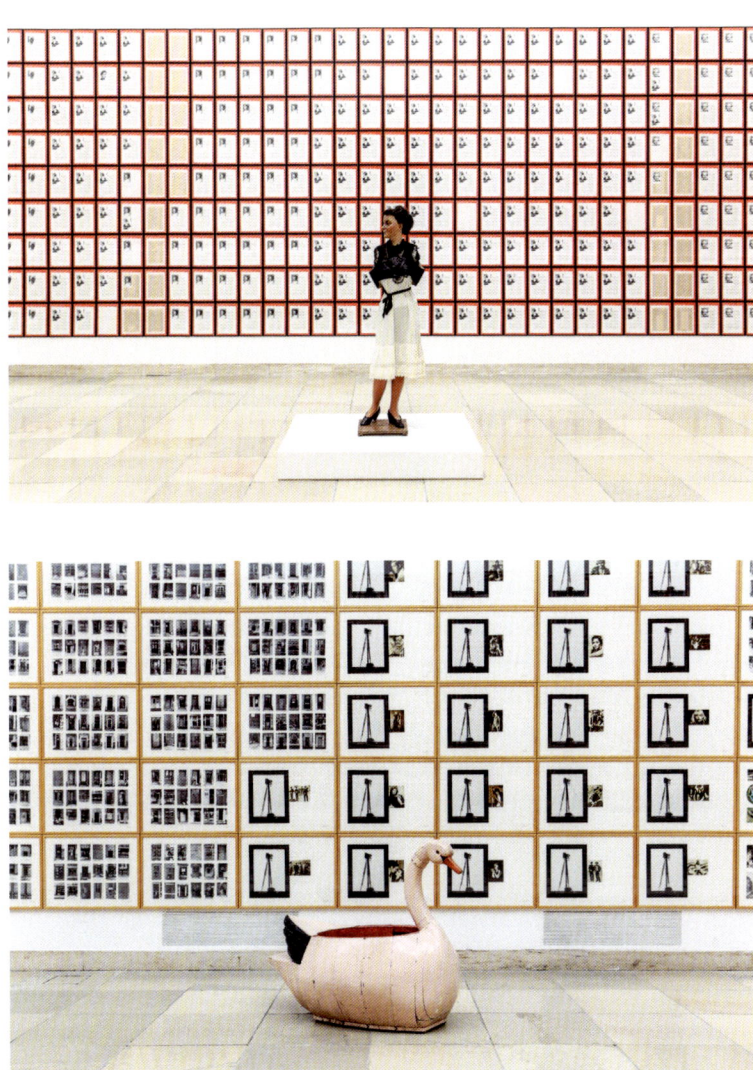

Quartett >88< , 1988. Haus der Kunst, 2015

Cultural History 1880–1983. Haus der Kunst, 2015

gong. And a Bible. There is an English-language Bible, which was opened to Isaiah, the prophet Isaiah. I'm given to understand, or I think—and I could stand corrected—that actually, it's the prerogative of the curator to open up the Bible. At the Dia installation, the book, the Bible, was opened, and then a page was turned every week for the duration of the exhibition. So there's no specific page that's specified by the artist. That's a clock that's in the show.

00:20:37:06

Darboven's art appears to be a direct confrontation with the seemingly infinite number of factors, both present and absent, at the creation of a work of art. Time and place, never fixed, not really, though dates can be appended, elements enumerated, sources authenticated, et cetera. Darboven's art appears to be the work of a mystic. I'm going to talk about mysticism in relationship to Darboven's work a little bit later. But right now, I'll just point out that it appears to me, or at least it lands on me, that part of Darboven's practice was mystical. I make this assertion solely based on Darboven's art, or my perception of it, and what and how I experience the artist's compositions. Nothing here spoken results from research into Darboven's biography. I could not figure out, or did not want to figure out, how I could fit Darboven's biography in relationship to this. There's something, again, deeply personal about my relationship to Darboven.

00:21:54:10

First, I wanted to talk about the experience of being at the Haus der Kunst. Jason Simon took this photo of me lost. Lost. Standing in the exhibition of *Cultural History*, I was struck with powerful feelings. A sense that there is an underlying order behind the overwhelming amount of stimuli—a queasy sensation of dread and excitement. Facing the immensity of ongoing world events, I felt small. It was like a Grand

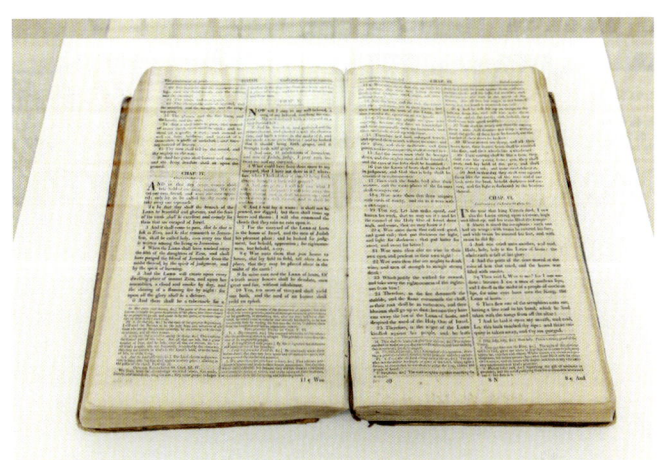

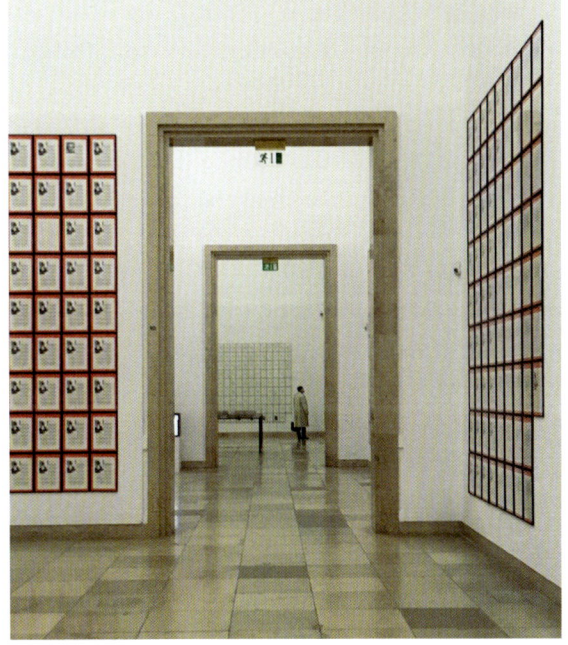

Cultural History 1880–1983. Detail: *Bibel* (bible)
Cultural History 1880–1983. Haus der Kunst, 2015. Photo: Jason Simon

Canyon moment. I felt insignificant. And with that came a kind of relief, a sense of freedom in my insignificance. And finally, I knew that I'm going to die. I felt my mortality. These sensations were powerfully felt. And these sensations, these powerful feelings, are the sensations we associate with Romanticism. And that's another claim I'm going to make. Darboven's art is a form of twentieth-century Romanticism.

00:23:15:25

As I said, it's very personal for me. This is an image of a book, *1975*. It's by Hanne Darboven. It's a rectangular book, bound on the shorter side of the width. It's about a half-an-inch thick. It's a calendar with the marks, the cursive marks that are associated with Darboven. I first encountered *1975* when I was the preparator at the Leo Castelli Gallery, 420 West Broadway, in 1985 or '86. At the time, I was twenty-one years old, an ambitious artist adopting the methods of Conceptual art, applying those methods to critiques of the very institutions, galleries, and museums that exhibited art. And I and many of my friends were most urgently interested in how these institutions assigned art value. Darboven's book, discovered in the library storage area at the Castelli Gallery, was a really important discovery for me. The book seemed appropriate to the context of the Castelli Gallery library. It shared the shelves with books by Ed Ruscha, Lawrence Weiner, Sol LeWitt, and many catalogues by artists preoccupied with words, marks, numbers, and systems—so-called Conceptual artists. I understood Darboven's book against that background, in that context, although I do not think Hanne Darboven was a Conceptual artist. Or rather, I think that that art historical term does not adequately describe her work.

00:25:10:00

1975, the book, made a deep impression. More emotional than cerebral, because it held open the promise of a mystery, using what

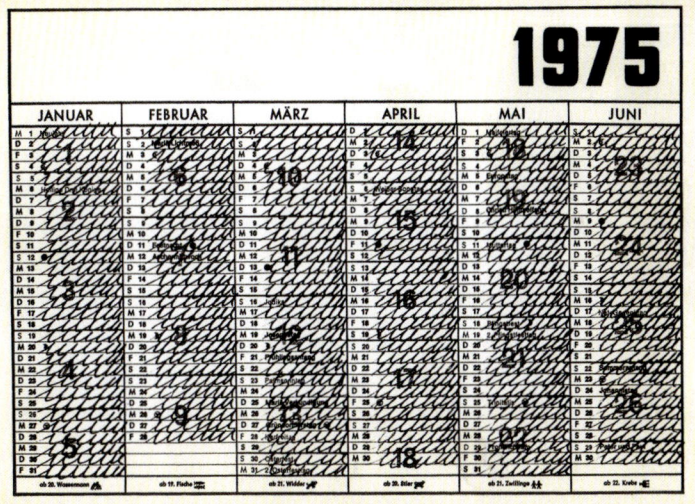

appeared to be a transparent system. A transparent system of composition contained within a preestablished bureaucratic form. My stint at Castelli as a preparator was preceded by two-and-a-half to three years of working as the assistant to the artist Joseph Kosuth. Deeply influenced by Kosuth at the time, I was introduced to the history of Conceptual art through him. And I took the job at Castelli at a moment of transition in my life. I was disillusioned by art, the art market, and art's failure to change an unjust world. I still believe that art can change the world. I was in the process, at that time, of abandoning art for activism. In particular, AIDS activism. Although I previously aligned my art with other social movements, it was AIDS activism that posed a dilemma for me—a kind of dilemma that's repeated throughout art history, at least in the modern period—to choose between art and action. I'll talk about that later. I don't know if I'm so convinced, at this moment in my life, that there is a choice to be made, or if there's ever a choice to be made, but we can debate it. We can talk about it. But at that time, I was very much convinced there was a choice to be made. Although the resolution for me was to make art about AIDS. And I will talk about my work in relationship to all of this.

00:26:50:18

In 1985, I was disenchanted with contemporary art and specifically Conceptual art, or how it developed throughout the seventies into the eighties—because of the tautological forms it took in many examples. Patterns and protocols followed to logical conclusions, within self-enclosed systems. Eventually, I applied these protocols to videos and writings directly tied to the AIDS activist movement, carrying forward what I could take from my youthful experiences in art. My disenchantment with Conceptual art in particular or art in general did not stem from Darboven's work, or the work of many other artists, particularly my peers. But with Conceptual art, I was particularly disappointed with the way in which tautology embraced the notion of the autonomy of the work of art. Even though the Conceptual artists went out into the world and used advertising as a trope within the language and conventions of their work, there seemed to me to be a leap, or a break, I needed to make at the time. This is all in retrospect. I think very differently now. Darboven's work never presented itself as a tautology to me. A tautology—a kind of very vulgar but simple way of explaining how I'm using the word tautology—is a self-defining, self-repeating, closed answer. So a good example of a tautology is when a child asks an adult or a figure of authority, "Why do I have to do this?" and the adult says, "Because I said so." That's the form of a tautology that I came to reject, one that closed me out as a viewer and asserted its own authority above my reading. I don't think Darboven's work ever did that. In fact, I think Darboven's work, if you look—and we'll talk more about *Cultural History*—does the opposite. One gets lost in its recursivity. I wouldn't call it tautological, I would call it recursive. It returns, but it always returns differently.

00:29:01:26

The difficulty with contemplating—Well, before I get to that, I want to talk a little bit about poetry. As I said, Darboven was very interested in poetry, and she even did a whole work devoted to Rilke's *Book of Images*. I wanted to point out some connections. Now this is fast forward. This is stuff I think about now. This is a poem by Lorine Niedecker, who was a twentieth-century American poet. She's identified with the Objectivist school of poetry, along with Zukofsky and Oppen and Reznikoff. She, too, wrote on calendars. And this is a series from 1935, where she filled a store-bought calendar with poems. "Wade all life backward to its source which runs too far ahead." "The satisfactory emphasis is on revolving. Don't send steadily; after you know me I'll be no one."

00:30:14:27

I'm very moved by Niedecker and her story. But this is not about Niedecker, so I'm not going to go too much into Niedecker's story or an analysis of these poems. It's interesting to note that she was an Objectivist, and the Objectivists were interested in reducing language to simplicity and to observation, and giving respect to the object beheld. And this seems consistent with Darboven's work, even though Niedecker is doing what Darboven refuses to do. Darboven wanted to write without describing. This is why she adopts math. That's a quote, "I want to write without describing." Math was pure, in Darboven's eyes. Math referred only to itself. And that is why she ends up making all of her work according to calculations and counting. So Niedecker is describing. But they are related, in some way—some ethereal way, maybe, in the ether, I mean—in that Objectivism has some relationship to the thingness in Darboven's work, or this preoccupation with thingness that occurs in visual art and poetry through successive stages of modernism, throughout the twentieth century.

00:31:38:23

1975 also makes me think a lot about Concrete poetry. And Darboven wanted to make time concrete. That's another quote. Darboven wanted to make time concrete. And I don't know, I have no way—none of the research that I've done leads me to any connection between Darboven and the Concrete poetry that was contemporary to her early work. But here is a poem by Carl Fredrik Reuterswärd. Excuse my pronunciation. "The Poem A." It's the letter *a* written over and over and over again. There is at least some simple resemblance to the marks that Darboven

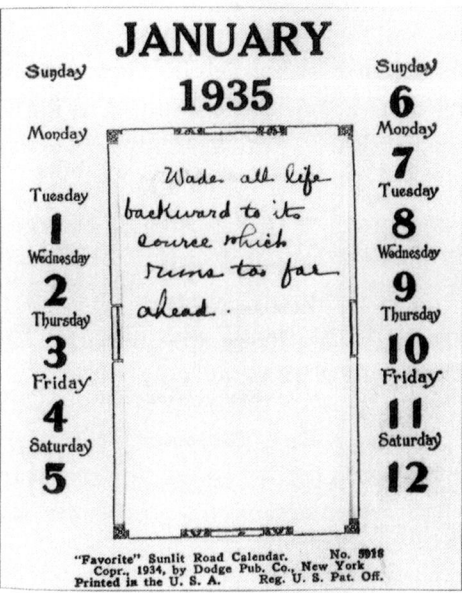

Wade all life / backward to its / source which / runs too far / ahead.

made. These are all from the fifties and early sixties. These would've been very much available, particularly in Europe and in the German-speaking world, although there was a huge Concrete poetry movement in Brazil. In fact, one of the most interesting things about Concrete poetry is, like Conceptual art, it emerged all over the world, all at once, in different forms. There's no way to really locate its origins. It's an international development in poetry. This is a poem by Gerhard Rühm, "The word imprisoned within itself." If you look at the center of the square, there's a *d*, there's the word *du*, which is "you," amid all the other letters. I included this because I think it's interesting. Maybe it's not adjacent to Darboven, but it's interesting to contemplate. This is Mary Ellen Solt, "Dogwood: First Movement." This is the first of three movements, 1966. It looks like a drawing of a flower, but actually, the outer petals are *w*'s, and at the center, there's enough *d*'s, *o*'s, and a *g* to make the word *dogwood* four times.

00:33:52:13

So there was a preoccupation in Concrete poetry with assigning numerical values to letters, to working with letters numerically. There's also a mystical tradition—I don't know if Darboven was aware of this at all, but—of assigning numerical values to letters in the alphabet, and then finding new meanings in words in the Torah, according to those numerical values. There are many different mystical traditions that use numbers and assign numerical values to the alphabet to create new meanings. This is a Dieter Roth Concrete poem, 1957, "Some variations on 4^4." I'm sorry, it's not a very good slide. It's lower-case *b*'s or *d*'s, *p*'s or *q*'s, each organized into patterns of four, in four to the fourth power. This is another Roth, "All as one? one as all?" the dot on the paper standing in for the one and the many, one as one, one as all.

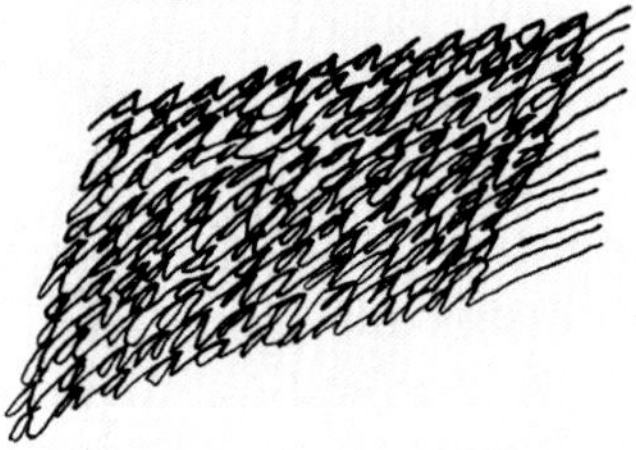

Carl Fredrik Reuterswärd, *"The Poem A"* (1954)

uuuuuuuuuuuuuuuuu
uuuuuuuuuuuuuuuuu
uuuuuuuuuuuuuuuuu
uuuuuuuuuuuuuuuuu
uuuuuuuuduuuuuuuu
uuuuuuuuuuuuuuuuu
uuuuuuuuuuuuuuuuu
uuuuuuuuuuuuuuuuu
uuuuuuuuuuuuuuuuu

Gerhard Rühm (1954)
The word imprisoned within itself.

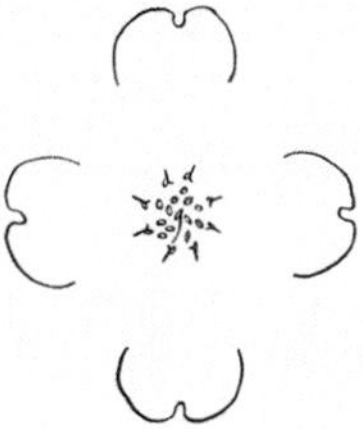

Mary Ellen Solt, "Dogwood: First Movement" (1966)
"According to legend the dogwood once grew as tall and strong as the oak. So to its great disgrace it was chosen as the tree most suitable for the Cross. Christ, though, pitied the tree in its shame and sorrow and performed the miracle of the dogwood. Henceforth, he said, it would grow short and crooked so that never again could it be used to such ignominious purpose. Each spring it would bear white flowers of four petals in the shape of the Cross with the crown of thorns at the center. And the tip of each petal would be notched and stained in memory of the nails and blood. 'Dogwood: Three Movements' attempts to relate the visual properties of the word to the shape of the flower as the symbol of suffering and its redemptive power, and to the laws of its growth in ascending planes of white." (M.E.S.)

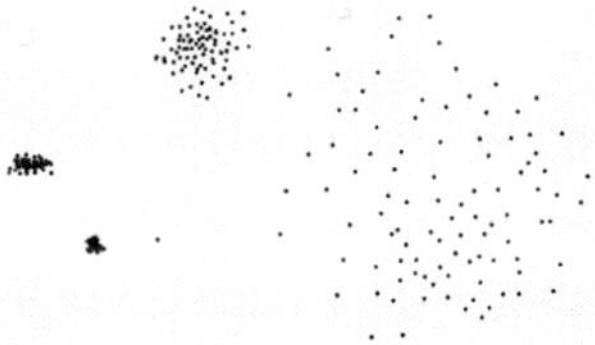

Diter Rot (1958)
"All as one? one as all?" (D.R.)
A prototype of non-semantic concretizing.

Carl Fredrik Reuterswärd, "The Poem A," 1954; Gerhard Rühm, "The word imprisoned within itself," 1954; Mary Ellen Solt, "Dogwood: First Movement," 1966; Dieter Roth, "All as one? one as all?" 1958

And these are working sheets. These are Darboven's. These were done in New York, 1965 to 1969. They were shown in a show of drawings, among drawings, or including drawings, by LeWitt and John Cage and others. Here, numerical values were used to generate line patterns. And this is where Darboven arrives at the notion of *Constructions*. These are called *Constructions*, and they're exhibited under that, as those. And this is one of the first times, or perhaps the first time, when Darboven starts presenting computation as work in and of itself, and/or the result of computation, the lines generated on the graphs. Can you see those? Kind of? Yeah? More computations. The computations get more evolved. I don't have time to go into each of these computations, but it's around this time that Darboven figures out how to numerically represent the calendar through addition, without referring to the specific century, so the calendar could repeat endlessly, without naming which specific century the date fell.

And these Constructions look a lot like Concrete poems. Especially that one. Here, time is made concrete. Numerical values are assigned spaces and proximities to create shades in a cube form. Here's what's at least convincing to me on the face of it: an intersection with Concrete poetry, Darboven's work, poetry, and visual art. I'm interested in the connection between visual arts and poetry historically. I had an epiphany in Vienna in 2008. I went to the Actionist show at MUMOK, the Museum of Modern Art in Vienna. And the whole basement was taken with this Actionist show, a historical Actionist show. And as you walked in, entered the show, there was one hallway of Concrete typewriter poetry on A4 paper. Gerhard Rühm was one of the figures, Ernst Jandl was another one. Just typewriter-written Concrete poetry and collages from magazines. And I swear, it was my experience that I could see all

Diter Rot (1957)
"Some variations on 4⁴." (D.R.)

Dieter Roth, "Some variations on 4^4," 1957
Konstruktion (*Construction*), 1965–69

of Actionism unfold from the Concrete poetry, the German-language Concrete poetry of that period, in that hallway. Then you turn and then you see all the famous Actionists and their work. But there, on the pages of the poetry, all the violence, all the compositional strategies, the relationship to language—it all fell into place, and I understood the procedures and protocols of Actionism. And then I was thinking about how the Lettrists preceded the Situationists, and how I love Surrealist visual art, but actually Surrealism was arguably primarily a literary movement. Literature and visual art have a deep, abiding connection, and I'm very interested in the ways that one could willfully misread visual art as poetry, as I did in my book *Imagevirus*. I willfully misread General Idea's *Imagevirus* logo as a Concrete poem. That's one example.

00:38:46:29

So the difficulty with contemplating Darboven's work arises because my own work as an artist and activist is currently subject to accumulating historical scrutiny. I have to say, this is a factor in my experience of contemplating Darboven. I experience a mixture of pride and dread as I witness my own past take concrete form in exhibitions, films, and books. Autobiography is primarily my chosen form, across various media. Autobiography is a means to establish coherence for a life composed of fits and starts, a personal history made of bits, pieces, parts, scattered across a field of debris. In many ways, the autobiographical form contrasts significantly with the elegant mathematical consistency of Darboven's records. I find it difficult, if not impossible to work like Darboven. I can't consider history with detachment in a purified language, using an overarching, increasingly complex system of categorization and taxonomy. I'm not sure that that's what Darboven is doing. Recall my Romantic experience with *Cultural History*. One can't append or attach specific meanings, explanations, interpretations to the specific objects of Darboven's installations. Considered together, all that stimuli

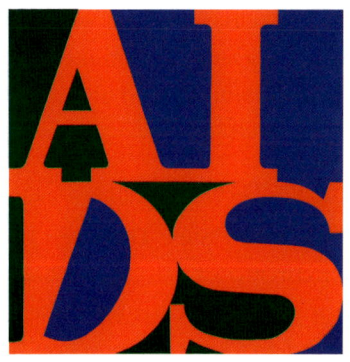

```
I    1 7 7 7 7 7 7 7 5 5 5 5 7 7 7 7 7 7 7 1
II   1 7 7 7 7 7 7 7 5 5 5 5 7 7 7 7 7 7 7 1
     1 7 7 7 7 7 7 7 5 5 5 5 7 7 7 7 7 7 7 1
     3 3 3 7 7 7 7 7 7 1 7 7 7 7 7 7 3 3 3 3
II   3 3 3 7 7 7 7 7 7 1 7 7 7 7 7 7 3 3 3 3
     3 3 3 7 7 7 7 7 7 1 7 7 7 7 7 7 3 3 3 3
     5 5 5 5 3 3 3 5 5 5 5 3 3 5 5 5 5 5 5 5
III  5 5 5 5 3 3 3 5 5 5 5 3 3 5 5 5 5 5 5 5
     5 5 5 5 3 3 3 5 5 5 5 3 3 5 5 5 5 5 5 5
     7 7 7 7 7 7 3 3 3 1 3 3 7 7 7 7 7 7 7 7
IV   7 7 7 7 7 7 3 3 3 1 3 3 7 7 7 7 7 7 7 7
     7 7 7 7 7 7 3 3 3 1 3 3 7 7 7 7 7 7 7 7
     5 5 5 5 3 3 3 5 5 5 5 3 3 5 5 5 5 5 5 5
V    5 5 5 5 3 3 3 5 5 5 5 3 3 5 5 5 5 5 5 5
     5 5 5 5 3 3 3 5 5 5 5 3 3 5 5 5 5 5 5 5
     3 3 3 7 7 7 7 7 7 1 7 7 7 7 7 7 3 3 3 3
VI   3 3 3 7 7 7 7 7 7 1 7 7 7 7 7 7 3 3 3 3
     1 7 7 7 7 7 7 7 5 5 5 5 7 7 7 7 7 7 7 1
VII  1 7 7 7 7 7 7 7 5 5 5 5 7 7 7 7 7 7 7 1
     1 7 7 7 7 7 7 7 5 5 5 5 7 7 7 7 7 7 7 1
```

General Idea, *AIDS*, 1987
Konstruktion (*Construction*), 1965–69

generates an overwhelming sensation. Her work, especially *Cutural History*, is about those overwhelming sensations—I admire Darboven's work, I respect it, and I'm grateful for it. I also approach it with envy and self-recrimination.

00:40:29:04

Aside from being a Romantic, Hanne Darboven is an Existentialist. Hanne Darboven is an Existentialist hero. According to Albert Camus, who I'm reading a lot of now—I think it makes sense to read Camus now, although Darboven didn't have a connection with Camus that I can find. Darboven did do a piece about Jean-Paul Sartre, and she quoted Sartre. But Camus is interesting to me now, and we could talk about that later, if you want. That's not the subject of this talk. However, I have been able to connect some of my reading in Camus, particularly *The Rebel*, to Darboven. "What is a rebel? A person who says no, but whose refusal does not imply a renunciation." A rebel also says yes from the first moment of rebellion. Darboven rejects description. She wrote without description. Darboven rejects arithmetic. Or rather, she preferred to use math for the purpose of counting, rather than to solve problems. In fact, this is taken from an interview with her. Math was a method of counting, a generator for the act of counting, which was the act of writing. That's not a quote, that's a paraphrase. Darboven's art does make sense within Camus's meditation on rebellion and style. This is a quote from Camus: "Whatever may be the chosen viewpoint of the artist, one principle remains common to all creators, stylization. Stylization supposes the simultaneous existence of reality and of the mind that gives reality its form. Through style, the creative effort reconstructs the world, and always with the same slight distortion that is the mark of both art and protest." This is true of Darboven's work. In Darboven's work, you see reality represented, and you also see the consciousness that is representing the reality, although you're not quite clear exactly

VII 1 2 3 4 5 6 7   (1xVII) I!reduziert

VI

V

IV

III

II

I

Konstruktionen (Constructions), 1965–69

the nature of that reality, its taxonomy, or the underlying intentions. I'll talk more about this later, but Darboven is quoted as saying, "My secret is that I have no secret." "My secret is that I have no secret."

00:43:03:10

Darboven's work is neither realism nor abstraction. Realism is enumeration, says Camus. True realism is enumeration of detail. But the flux and flow of life is constant, and too large to be captured in all its details. True abstraction is not possible either. A pure abstraction does not exist in art, because there is no way to avoid reference or frame. We are limited in our capacities to comprehend reality in its full complexity altogether. And we cannot create what does not exist. At the outer edges of experimentation, we can discover previously incomprehensible phenomena only when conditions allow for their appearances. So what's discovered might've been there, but was not visible, except for a set of circumstances that allows it to become visible, including our presence and also the tools of measurement that are employed. The problem or crisis of artistic creation is resolved through style, as Camus talks about style. It is the sensibility in which both maker and receiver find refuge. Gertrude Stein taught us that nothing changes but the thing seen, and that changes the composition. So what's apprehended is what gives form to what is seen. Stein is very important to Darboven. And I think Stein is important to Darboven in a number of ways. First, because Darboven makes a piece about Stein. But also because I'm very interested in the way that Stein is taken up by the Conceptual artists. A lot of people claim lineage to Stein within the Conceptual art movement; but they see her as a systems builder—perhaps Mel Bochner and others. I'm not saying they're wrong; this is just a matter of interpretation. Carl Andre will refer to Stein and talk about systems. And if you look at their work, and that of others who claim lineage to Stein, it's a numerical generation of systems. Whereas another epiphanic experience I had in

Vienna was reading *The Making of Americans*, by Gertrude Stein, where I realized that the rhythms in Stein are not numerical. They're not systematized according to math. They arise according to the body's drives. The repetitions could be both analog and digital, but they're the analog and digital processes that overlap within the body. How does the analog and digital happen within the body? I'll explain very quickly. If you read Anthony Wilden's book *System and Structure*—I discovered it in Kosuth's library around 1984. Well, the book was published in 1973; I was only nine in 1973. But Kosuth had it, I read it. In *System and Structure*, Wilden says, look at the structure of the neuron. It's both an analog and digital formation. An analog decision is a decision between too much and too little. So what's happening with the nerves and the neurons is that the dendrites are sensing thresholds of too much or too little of a hormone, let's say, or the presence of chemicals in the body. What happens when either too much or too little occurs is that a switch goes off and a yes/no decision is made, whether the neuron fires or not. The neurons firing, the yes/no decision, that's a digital process. And when you get that cascade of firing, you have decisions made within the body. But the analog and the digital occur biologically within the body physically as part of a complex process. Understanding the analog and the digital as two kinds of decision-making involved in a feedback loop—that kind of upends all of the debates we've had over the past twenty years about analog versus digital mediums, film versus video, et cetera. We can talk more about that after.

00:47:14:02

But that's what I thought about Stein, that this was about thresholds. This was about recursivity. This was about a body writing. And I tried to emulate that in some writing that I'm going to show you when I talk about my own work. The Existential dimension I locate in Darboven's work is drawn from my reading Camus—It's not sufficient to live. There must be a destiny that does not have to wait for death. It is therefore justifiable to say that people have an idea of a better world than this. Better does not mean different, it means unified. This passion which lifts the mind above the commonplaces of the dispersed world from which it nevertheless cannot free itself, this is the passion of unity. And I'm going to make a distinction here between totality and unity. And this is very important to Camus, but it's also important to understanding Darboven's work. In Darboven's work, we experience the passion for unity, I identify here as a flow. Totality is the reduction of everything to one. And *The Rebel* is interesting to read now, because it's about rebellion producing both great beauty and great horror. It's that moment in the middle of the twentieth century, just after the war, when Camus is understanding that the rebel—the creative person—has an impulse to protest against death. And that protest leads to a desire for order and the development of a totality, a comprehensible totality, right? Which is a protest against the inevitable. That protest, rebellion, often leads to genocide, as we know. Right? So he's distraught. Camus was deeply ambivalent about the rebellious impulse. And he understands that the rebellious impulse must be contained and understood within the limits of mortality, and that must find form in style. That's where it finds form, in style and sensibility.

00:49:40:15

When I face Hanne Darboven's installations, I feel that passion, that desire for unity. I feel it in my body. I don't know if it's a property of the work. I draw a distinction between totality and unity, as I've already done. *Cultural History* poses the problem of unity, and so do other works by Darboven. And when I listen to Darboven's musical compositions, I can begin to imagine, to sense the accord that unity stimulates.

Let me just play you a piece of Darboven's music. She wrote music. She would make computation, and then assign numerical values to notes, and generate the music that way. This is *Opus 17A*, produced immediately after finishing *Cultural History*. I'm just going to play you a section of it. I'm a filmmaker among other jobs. And in the Haus der Kunst, there were headphones all over the gallery, so you could listen to Darboven's many musical compositions. Never in my life would I imagine that this would be the soundtrack to Darboven's work. If I was going to shoot a film, this would not be the music. [*laughter*]

00:51:17:02

[*music plays*] BORDOWITZ: It's a fantastic piece of music. It's one hour and eight minutes. Dia produced a disc of it. And it's worthwhile listening to it and all of her music. A lot of it's on the web, too. I'm just getting back to my slideshow here. One second.

00:52:57:08

Now I'm going to switch gears a bit and talk about my own work. And I never really thought this through, but like I said, Darboven's been an abiding influence. Kosuth, still somewhere in the back of my head, remains an influence. He taught me a lot about what it meant to be an artist and a lot about what it meant to make art. Even though I had that departure from a certain way of thinking, Darboven doesn't seem to fall into those same areas of difficulty for me. However—Oh, that's not what I wanted. [*BORDOWITZ loses his place in the PowerPoint.*] Oh, we're going to have to fast-forward through all of this because somehow, I lost—This is what the film would look like. [*BORDOWITZ speeding through the PowerPoint.*]

00:53:53:00

That's the editing room diagram from my film *Fast Trip, Long Drop*. I drew that in the editing room, when I was editing that fifty-five-minute film, and then I had it rendered by somebody, because it was a little bit too sloppy and I wasn't necessarily interested in my own handwriting. It's three clock faces touching each other at different junctures. And the structure of *Fast Trip, Long Drop*, I won't show you the film or a clip of it. You can see the film. It's distributed by Video Data Bank; it's also on the web. And it was showing recently in the *Greater New York* exhibition at PS1. The diagram and the film, it's like old television watching; it's three spins around the dial, that has a reversible entry and exit point. And I realized that even when I started making and after I made AIDS activist video for a long time, and *Fast Trip, Long Drop* was a return, after six years of only making collaborative work—from 1987 to 1993, I only made work with other video AIDS activists, and primarily Jean Carlomusto, for the Gay Men's Health Crisis. We had a television show. So I didn't make any work under my own signature. In 1993, I felt like I wanted to—I was also very sick at the time. This is before protease inhibitors. I have AIDS, as many of you know. And so I actually really thought *Fast Trip, Long Drop* was going to be my last film. And so I wanted to say some things that I didn't really want anyone else to be burdened with saying. So I went into the editing room and thought a lot about time and mortality and working against the clock. Which is something I respond to in Darboven's work. I'm sure it's there. She talks about the concretization of time. She says her work is very Existential. There is a discussion about Romanticism in interviews with Darboven. This is not strange to Darboven scholarship.

00:56:05:10

This is from *Volition*. But I'm not going to read this because I'm going to read something else from *Volition*, and perhaps end there or show something else. But *Volition* was, is, a book I wrote in Vienna. I spent every day writing questions. The entire book is composed of questions. It was the year that I gave up on answers, and I have not recovered.

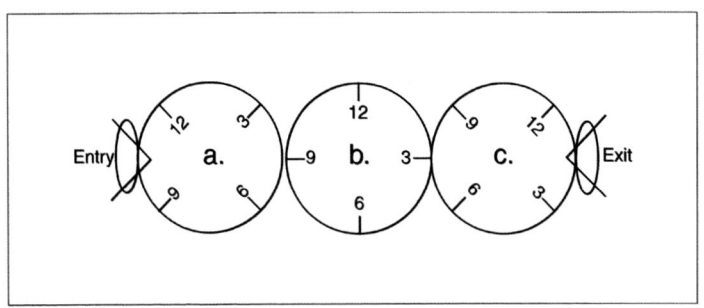

I wrote it as I imagine Stein wrote—with the body. On one level, it's an homage to smoking, because at that point in Vienna, you could still smoke with impunity, everywhere—elevators. That's a correct locution, to smoke with impunity? That means you could smoke anywhere, right?

MAN: Right.

00:56:57:03

BORDOWITZ: So I was just sitting in Thomas Bernhard's café and writing questions, chain smoking. And sometimes I could go for twenty questions and then I'd run out of steam and light another cigarette. And then I would just be desperate for a question and I would write something like, what are the last four digits of your Social Security number? Which is a question I'm asked almost daily. And then I would start again. I published the entire book as it was written. I didn't change the order or anything. And it ends in fits and starts, and I just started every day where I left off. So Hanne Darboven says, "My secret is that I have no secret." Now she's not the only one who's said that. I've seen that in a lot of different contexts. One could read that in an antihumanist way. By that, I mean like an Althusserian way. Again, it's late and I don't want to unpack a lot at the moment. One could just say that it's antihumanist, it rejects the existence of a soul. Or perhaps rejects the notion that the eyes are windows to a soul. Or perhaps it critiques the assumption that we're unique or in some way singular in terms of the ways we appear or the ways we write. That's one way of understanding Darboven's refusal or complication of the secret. "My secret is that I have no secret." I wrote about secrets, too, in *Volition*. And so now I'm going to read you a section from *Volition*, the book of questions.

00:58:55:01

Is it possible that some portion of ourselves remains a secret from ourselves?
Is it possible that some portion of ourselves remains a secret from others?

What does it mean now to be an artist in the 21st century?
What does anything mean now if nothing means anything
at all?
Does nothing mean anything at all?
How can anything mean something as a reflection without
being?
Is it possible to become reflection without being?
How does the question of being possess urgency at the
moment?
How is meaning being and being nothing something anytime
soon but not now?
What is the question now?
How?
How do I proceed now in a way that recalls what it was to
proceed before proceeding was a question?
How could proceeding be a question other than what I have
posed just now?
Which principle must I combine with what difficulty to make
a virtue?
How is virtue appreciated now?
How is quality achieved?
Is quality achieved as a matter of volition?
Is volition a cause or an effect, both or neither?
Does anything at all originate with me?
In what sense am I original?
How is originality a principle?

Can originality be encompassed by anything other than the
concept itself?
When we say that something is original what are we saying?
What are we feeling?
How does saying coincide with feeling?
Are saying and feeling two distinct movements?
Is it possible for an inanimate object to say anything?
Is it possible for an object to possess feeling?
How is possession felt and feeling possessed?
Is emotion an object to have and to share?
If we are both sad looking at the same thing, like a painting,
can we say that our sadness is one substance of which we both
partake?
Is sadness a principle or an element?
How do we breathe as we feel?
What do we gain by saying an object, the object, any object,
possesses nothing intrinsically?
What do we gain by saying that no object exists unless we
create it for ourselves?
Can we share what we ourselves do not create?
Who are we that we create as we share without volition?
What do we gain by saying we lack volition?
How do we repeat ourselves?
What is the question of belief?
Do I believe?
How do I believe?

Gregg Bordowitz, from *Volition*, 2009

Is it possible that these two portions, secret from ourselves and secret from others, are not identical, they are different portions of a self? Is the secret a structural feature of the person? Is consciousness a permeable barrier regulating the flow of stimuli between an imagined inside and a projected outside? Where is the secret?

I think the secret is structural. Which doesn't make it any less soulful.

Is it possible that I am only a means? A means of what? Am I a means to an end that exceeds the totality of my senses, a sum that's never totaled?

That's how I think about Darboven's work. It's a sum that never totals; but there is always a flow of unity. I'm going to stop there. [*applause*]

* * *

The talk was followed by a question-and-answer period. Included below are partial answers to questions that were edited out of this transcription.

01:00:31:18

BORDOWITZ (Cont.): Thank you. I would like to converse with you, if you would like to converse with me. I think we're going to have lights.

01:02:36:21

One of the things about *Cultural History* and all of Darboven's work is that you can lamp on certain things, and then you realize you're lamping on things that produce responses in you. So as I'm walking through *Cultural History*, I see Mao, I see the *Red Brigade,* I see all these covers from *Der Spiegel* from the seventies. But I'm ignoring the pictures of soccer players and the pictures of the Alps. And I realized that what Darboven is doing is producing a field through which one finds hooks, or rather one gets caught by particular lures. The objects, the sculptural works within the installation are nodes, or places or vantages, from which to view the panels, as well. They also add scale. They're all human scale, in some ways. And actually, as you could see, you can only see like four of the panels, if you're looking eye level, because they far exceed one's height, and unless you want to get down on your knees, you can't really see what's below. And so what you're left with is this kind of overwhelming Romantic feeling that I talked about. Obviously, Romanticism plays a very strong and problematic role in German history. And there are pictures of soldiers. There's a picture of Hitler. I was trying to think, is this postwar work? Well, chronologically, it is. But how is it postwar work?

01:05:52:05

I've been resisting a reading of the work as originating in trauma specifically tied to the historical event of the Holocaust. I've been resisting looking at Darboven's work as only postwar work, or reducing it—I'm afraid of it being reduced to that—because I see these tendencies, first of all, in bureaucratic culture, which takes over in the twentieth century, from industrialization through postindustrialized modes of production. And you can think about Max Weber and later thinkers, theorists who understand the bureaucratization and increasing instrumentalization of all of our lives under capitalism. It plays itself out specifically in Germany. We know the history. But I think I resist a reductive reading—I'm not arguing against it, but I resist the reduction. I couldn't say it myself. I still can't rest easily saying that Darboven's work is postwar work especially about the trauma of the Holocaust, simply because the work is more complicated. It can be interpreted as being about bureaucracy or counting. Because as I showed, like the history of Concrete poetry, which is entirely preoccupied with counting syllabics, counting letters, numerical values; and the mystical Jewish tradition that I talked about, which is preoccupied with assigning numbers and using computation as meaning-generating devices. The protocols and procedures in Darboven's works are too pervasive, drawn from a broad range of history too vast to be reduced to a reading of Darboven as a postwar artist. Now, she is a postwar artist chronologically, historically. She's also making work about the Enlightenment and industrialization and bureaucratization—I don't know how account for it all.

01:10:45:05

Obviously, it is work that draws on the German language and is made by a German artist. I don't want to argue but I want to resist, the way in which trauma can be easily placed at the center of the secret. Or a specific historical trauma. I believe that all artists are enacting trauma. Not specific historical trauma, necessarily, but trauma that is the very foundation of our psyche. I'm indebted to and invested in psychoanalytic theory, and I believe that the psyche is formed on trauma and contradiction. And Camus—I brought that in because the basic trauma that we all face is that we realize we're going to die. I mean, the existential conundrum of knowing that you're going to die is trauma enough. Right? So yes, of course, there are historical coordinates to this trauma and we can identify specific traumas. And maybe—someone mentioned AIDS. You know, I think about the way in which AIDS—having AIDS, writing about AIDS, making art about AIDS—affects the work. And maybe this is just a block on my part, but when I'm sitting in the editing room, when I sat in the editing room with *Fast Trip* and was drawing that diagram, I was thinking formally, but I don't know—

01:12:50:28

All I'm trying to say is that maybe I'm blocked around this. I personally cannot sit here and locate Darboven's trauma. I cannot attribute sole explanatory force to the history of World War II or to the Holocaust. I resist that.

I don't have the skills or there's something in me that resists fully assigning explanatory force to one particular event, even though that event is so daunting and huge in Darboven's history and our history. What does it mean to be a formalist? is an interesting question, because of the way we're talking about different kinds of formalism—tautology versus recursivity, referentiality versus non-referentiality. I think Darboven defeats all of those things. And I think that's why we still look at Darboven's work, because she defeats these distinctions between realism and abstraction. She uses formalism as a generator for a very powerful experience that doesn't close in around itself, but rather produces either awe or dread, or both—Or a sense of humor, yeah, I feel that Darboven's work is funny because I fail it. I utterly fail it. Because it's incomprehensible. It just makes one—When I recently visited *Cultural History* in Munich, I saw things that made me laugh; but then I also saw things that horrified me. It's a really horrifying piece. What's very brave about Darboven is she is truly producing—she's not cherry picking, she's truly producing—an archive to contemplate both the sublime and the ridiculous, including beauty, violence, trivial details, and within that continuum to contemplate colonialism and racism, and give you a purchase from which to mobilize one's own thoughts. And that's what's most amazing about *Cultural History*, is that there are some very difficult things to encounter. There are things that are ludicrous, like seeing an image of the Red Brigade on the cover of *Der Spiegel* next to a soccer player. One could walk in there and say, oh, this is relativizing, in the way that our world is relativizing, and horrifyingly so, in that horrors come up against silliness all the time and it's hard to focus. In this, she's not alone. You know, the Surrealists were interested in early mail-order shopping catalogues for the same reason, right? It was the first time in that particular area of the world where you saw images of corsets next to images of iron stoves, right? This kind of relativizing, this kind of—If you're a Marxist, as I am, you think it's the devaluing of use value in favor of exchange value. And what you see in Darboven's work is also this swapping out of use value for exchange value, but a return to a possible different usage of the object and the material that's presented. An alternative way of visiting history or revisiting history. But you're thrust back upon yourself. Or at least that was my experience.

01:19:54:18

And I'll tell you the truth, I'm not against talking about artists' biographies in work. In my General Idea book, I interviewed AA Bronson. I'm not concerned about bringing art history too close to sociology. I'm not even an art historian, you know, so I don't really have to operate by disciplinary rules anyway. But in this instance I chose not to include any of it in any explanatory way, because I don't want to pathologize the work, nor do I want to append any psychoanalytical reading of the artist. If I were going to talk about obsession or obsessional neuroses in Conceptual art, or some tendencies in art, I could do that without discussing Darboven as an example. How does obsessional neurosis manifest in Conceptual art in general?—that's interesting. But we don't have time for that. [*laughter*] Nor maybe do I have the chops. What I want to do is express my gratitude to all of you. Thank you very much for your generosity and for being here. [*applause*]

01:21:29:28

[END]

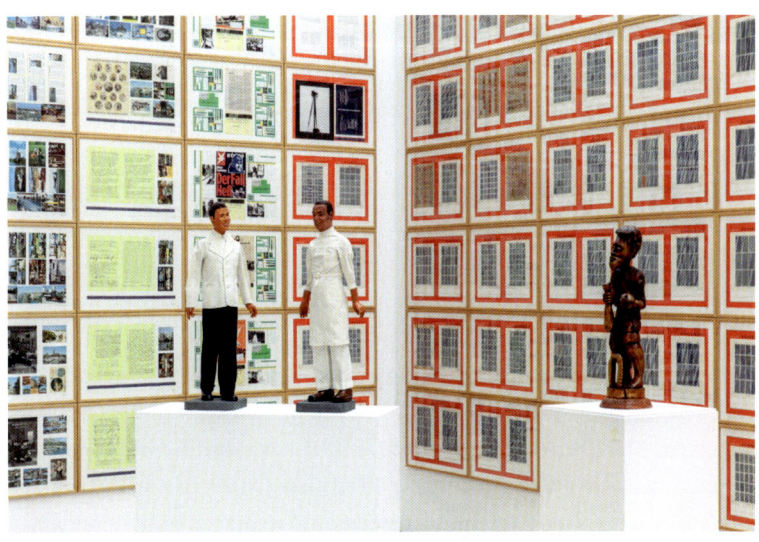

Cultural History 1880–1983. Haus der Kunst, 2015

Sam Lewitt
No More Words

The women say that, with the world full of noise, they see themselves already in possession of the industrial complexes. They are in the factories, aerodromes, radio stations. They have taken control of communications.   —Monique Wittig, *Les Guérillères*

This drawing was contributed to a 1749 book called *Mémoire sur la réformation de la police de France*, written by a gendarme who gives his name as M. Guillaute and illustrated by Gabriel de Saint-Aubin. It makes a mammoth proposal for a state-sponsored paper-processing machine. The drawing depicts a comprehensive system of urban surveillance that would use preprinted forms to register the name, age, address, birthplace, travels, employment history, rent due, and tax status of every resident and visitor in the city. He invented this machine to store and retrieve these forms with rapid efficiency: "vertical wheels twelve feet in diameter would rotate to reveal horizontal shelves full of files. The clerks would access these storage devices from wall terminals, controlling them with foot pedals. Each one would be able to hold more than one hundred thousand of Guillaute's forms."[1]

The state's desire for an overview of the practices, locations, and debts of every individual, in all its telling detail, is certainly not unfamiliar to us denizens of a technically saturated culture, which facilitates international surveillance programs, optimizes search analytics, and mostly voluntary submissions of every detail of our lives that can be broadcast. The scope of this ambition has only extended to increasingly unprecedented proportions. The Stasi, for example, headquartered 48,000 filing cabinets containing detailed information

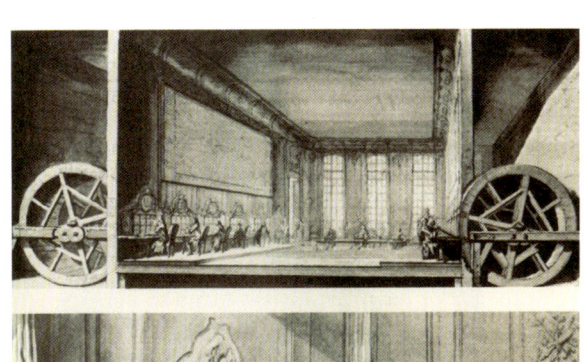

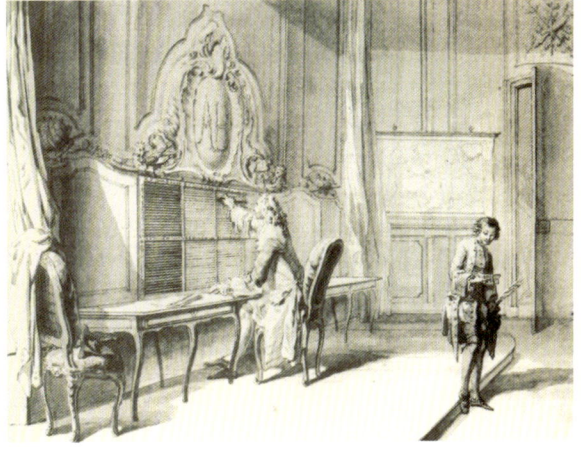

Gabriel de Saint-Aubin, "The Paperholder," 1749

of the goings-on of the citizens of the German Democratic Republic. Each of the Stasi's cabinets contained an average of about sixty files (equal to roughly 30,000 pages). This would correspond in digital terms to about 120MB of data. The National Security Agency's recently opened data center in Utah is capable of storing up to 5 zettabytes (5 billion terabytes). If printed out, the stored information would fill about 42 trillion filing cabinets.

But the mere quantity of data, while perhaps shocking, is simply a technical determination, a question of computational processing power. The leap to a truly unprecedented quality of experience within this scenario is the degree to which quantitative accumulations of data necessitate wholesale transformations in the meaning of literacy. Literacy emerges as a deeply historical and political determination of the subject's capacity or incapacity to lay claim to intelligibility via techniques of information handling.

What is interesting about Guillaute's relatively tiny operation and its clerks, as illustrated here, is the stark contrast between the massive post-humanist surveillance and information processing plant, and the very human scale of the clerk's office. The office just barely masks the enormous racks of data with a skein of elegant wallpaper and stately plaster ornament. While today's doyens of financial and state authority would never dream of draping garlands around their servers, which hold our criminalizing data and records—shrouding them instead in impenetrable brick-and-mortar structures with unlisted addresses— this shouldn't blind us to the real import of the drawings in the present. As Ben Kafka notes:

> What makes Saint-Aubin's images so revealing . . . is not their success, either as art or as technical illustration, but their failure. The disruptive potential of the new mechanisms is not quite contained by the aristocratic social relations that Saint-Aubin so carefully encoded in the office's airy

bright aesthetic. The heavy wheels appear to be on the verge of crushing the fragile space and the order that it represents.[2]

At the tipping point of political modernity that these illustrations inhabit, the contradictions of paperwork as facilitator and expression of a systematic attempt to gain a positive overview, masked in the finery of protecting the social order, are as persistent as any. If the seeds of progressive Enlightenment rationality were planted in the eighteenth century, so were the reactionary mechanisms that relied on similar comprehensive systems of recording, storing, and transmitting all available empirical data about the world. It is not a coincidence that the first volumes of Denis Diderot's *Encyclopédie* started to appear one year after Guillaute's data storage program was publicly proposed. Today it would seem that the mechanisms of information availability and total surveillance have finally collapsed: fused into unreadable writing, housed in an environment that has converted the position of the clerk into that of the security guard and IT specialist.

To speak of it a little abstractly, there are two basic ways to understand systematicity as—whatever else it signifies—the production of a general and generic framework for conceptualizing particulars: either the overviewing system's subsumption of particulars is understood as a relation of heteronomy—as a relationship of domination; or forms of relation are understood to be enabled that would otherwise remain dumbly caught in simple self-identity without their being brought systematically in line. In either case, the system is understood to have a formalized structure whose intelligibility extends from the fact that it describes some level of *paradigmatic* regularity and *syntagmatic* integrity: an axiom-driven formula, a model of the solar system, a thermodynamic machine, German Idealism, the difference between what we understand by the word "Dia" and the word "walrus," historical arrangements of individual or social reproduction and accumulation. Systematicity operates by virtue of modeled norms, which are the conditional ground for determining functional roles and behavioral tendencies that can be tracked as having a certain consistency in logic, especially through time.

ANOTHER KIND OF OFFICE

I

This will be a highly selective and tangential commentary on Hanne Darboven's work. I have come to understand *Kulturgeschichte 1880–1983* (*Cultural History 1880–1983*, 1980–83) as constituting its own kind of paper-processing machine, but one that contradicts and short-circuits the functional integration of elements into systematic coherence. In what follows, I will allow myself to get detoured, to be led down paths that are sometimes only indirectly situated to the major themes of Darboven's project, but which I hope produce connections within a constellation that her work configures for me. I'm tempted to say that what interests me in Darboven's work is not exactly the major themes per se, but the manner in which questions of language and calculation, time and labor, historical catastrophe and recollection, become thematically major through very minor, detailed, peculiar operations that are eccentrically subsumed into larger organizational principles and graphic expressions. In particular, it is the attendant difficulties involved in describing what exactly it *is* that is organized and graphically expressed that keeps me interested, as well as somewhat mystified. I am going to allow anachronism, interpretive leaps, digressions, and abrupt appearances of peripheral actors to give the content of this discussion, since those operations have been what have held my attention for some time now.

II

I am not sure when I first learned about Darboven's work, but the first major installation I saw of hers was undoubtedly *Cultural History*, not

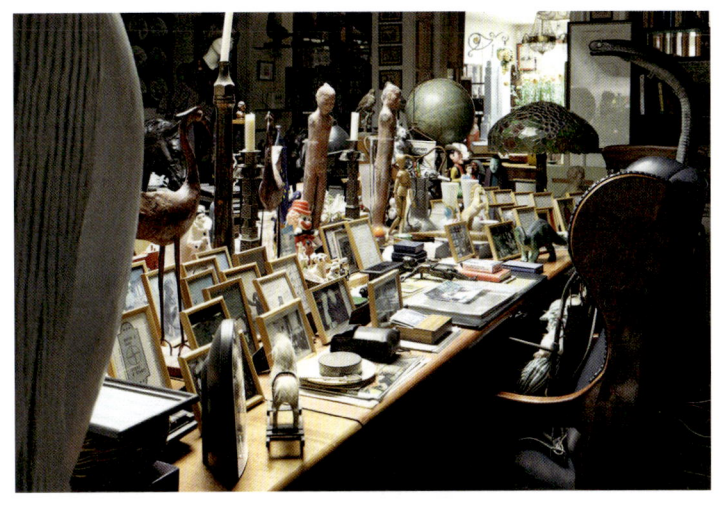

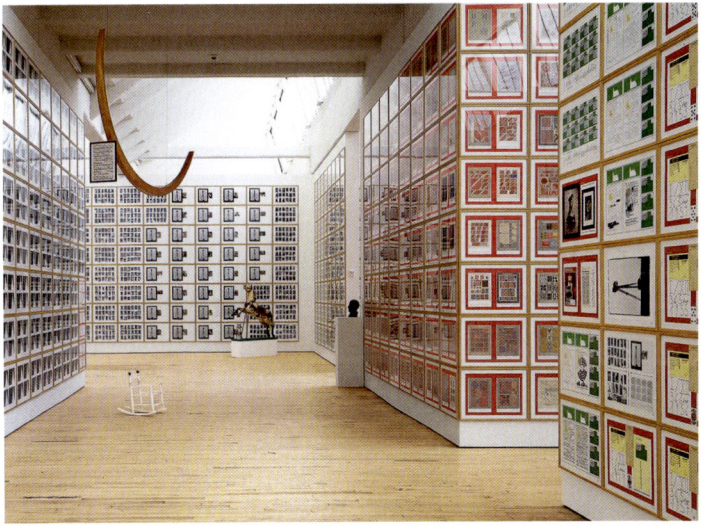

Annex, Am Burgberg, Hamburg-Rönneburg, 2013
Cultural History 1880–1983, 1980–83. Dia:Beacon, Beacon, New York, 2003

long after the opening of Dia:Beacon, Beacon, New York, in 2003 upon visiting the site for the first time while still an undergraduate student. This work inhabits a unique place in Darboven's collection of "writings," which is how she referred to her works. *Cultural History* is massive. Unlike other modes of working prior to it, the work is not composed primarily of numerical sequences drawn from the calendar, as her *Konstruktionen (Constructions)* from the 1960s are; nor does it focus on any historical or proper name as a touchstone or dedication, as her writings from the 1970s on sometimes do. Whereas in the latter works, the figures that she chooses as proper names inhabit both monumental and marginal places within the history of the Enlightenment (such as Johann Wolfgang von Goethe, Gottfried Wilhelm Leibniz, Niels Bohr—but also figures like Johann Jacob Moser, who invented an early filing system of cataloguing references, and who was referenced in Darboven's 1975 work *Card Index: Filing Cabinet*), *Cultural History* seems to take the historical trajectory of Enlightenment itself as a fraught subject, one which does not retrieve great names of the past and present, but filters the project of the disenchantment of knowledge and the rationalization of reason through indigent details and catastrophic turns.

As first encounters go, what I remember was certainly being impressed by the work's immense shifts in scale, between its environmental envelope of information and its discrete details. The work is a sort of graphic environment that is animated by the viewer's passage through it. Viewers are shuttled through both extended repetitions of images and abrupt shifts between modes of communication, such as postcards, photographs, book pages, plastic mannequins, and plaster busts, among other items. The layering of media that this is conducted through supports heterogeneous graphic modes—texts and signs of different order are crashed together, requiring different types of literacy to operate simultaneously. Most of this material is assembled from German and American contexts of twentieth-century mass culture, paired with nineteenth-century keepsakes and popular artifacts. (Boredom is surely not far beneath these layers.) Strictly considered on an optical level, Darboven administered these components from what she once referred to as her "scrap paper economy" into an equally serialized and turbulent semiotic space. This economy hangs together as a perceptual experience of interruption. It is as if the cumulative effect is to annotate the linear dash that separates the dates in the work's title with discontinuities and halts, culled from the communication techniques of a culture irretrievably scarred by the caesura and catastrophes of the development of Enlightenment rationality into technologically advanced war and mass-cultural social management.

What I also remember from my first experience entering—or trying to enter—the work, on a strictly subjective level, was the distinct feeling of what I can only call defensive fatigue. The sort of strange psychic enervation that is pleated with both excitement and anxiety, an anticipatory resistance that I can relate perhaps to a primitive reflex for self-preservation. This usually occurs in front of phenomena that I know are simply too interesting to deal with. This is to say, the sheer task of entering the work made a claim on me, and practices that send me down these kinds of rabbit holes tend to be the ones that make the strongest claims and have the force of real ambivalence. This relationship with artworks tends to be both irritating and intense, causing bouts of procrastination and fits of laughter in the face of something that seems inexhaustible. But I find myself drifting back to this kind of work.

On the most basic level, I find myself at a loss to describe the work to myself. A work like *Cultural History*, despite its unique status in Darboven's cumulative writings, shares with earlier works the trait of having a clearly defined structure, which is rigidly spelled out in the "index" section of the work (a section of panels that lists all of the artwork's objects). It also has an articulate, if complex, syntactical clarity, which is visually accessible in its alternating red-and-green, black-and-white templates and double-page layouts. Yet the scope of its material is expansive to say the least, constituting a collection of mercurial and marginal images and texts, objects and utterances that are sometimes clearly related to the span of dates in the work's title, and in some cases only gnomically hint at their historical specificity. To get a sense of a more successful possibility for the work's description, I'd like to quote at length Michael Newman's concise but methodical account of *Cultural History*'s general structure. The work is composed of 1,590 framed panels and nineteen objects. It includes an:

> [overwhelming] variety of material incorporated into them: postcards and pictures of toy gifts; reproductions of Darboven's own work and that of others; magazine covers; pages of catalogues and found fabric patterns; a collection of German cigarette cards from the time of World War I; page after page of Darboven's cursive "writings"; sheets of music; calendars; numerical calculations; and portrait photographs. Then, there are the freestanding objects, attractive and appalling, puzzling and kitschy: a doll with a teddy bear, models of human figures, shop-window mannequins, a Bible, and a gong among them. . . .

> Panels of pre–World War II postcards are followed by a section of reproductions of earlier installations by Darboven from books and catalogues. . . . [Then on to] the streets of New York . . . using photographs of Manhattan doorways by Roy Colmer, as well as panels of publicity shots of movie and rock stars. Presented together with a photograph of a large-format camera on a tripod, and concluding with a photograph of a light bulb. . . . After this American interlude, the Federal Republic of Germany returns in a sequence of covers of the popular Left-ish news periodical *Der Spiegel*, combined in panels with postwar postcards. . . .

> This section is followed by a collection of pages from a pattern book for textile designs that Darboven purchased during her time in New York in

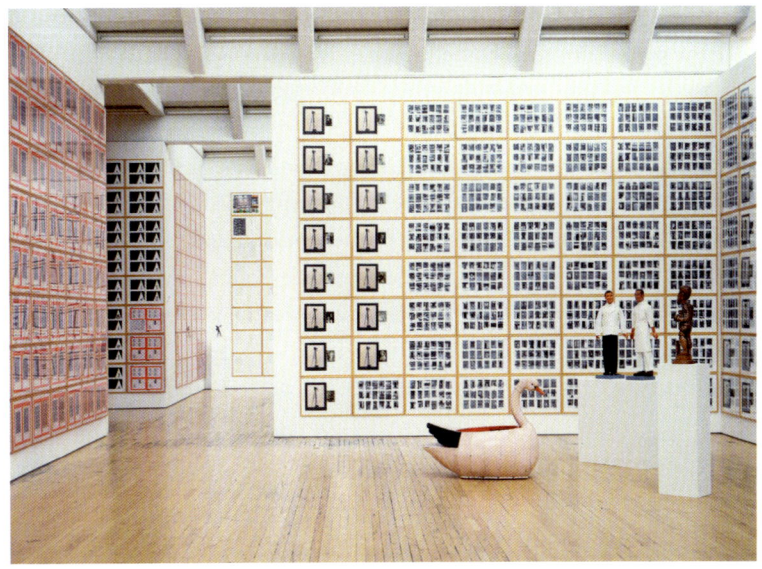

Cultural History 1880–1983. Dia:Beacon, 2003

the 1960s. . . . As if to connect technology and war, these patterns are followed by panels of German collectors' cards from the World War I period, including racist depictions of "our enemies."

The following section jumps ahead past the 1960s, with sheets from the catalogue of the Ludwig Collection. . . . This . . . is then contrasted with the mass reproduction of high art in pages from a Deutsche Bank calendar featuring German Romantic watercolors.

The penultimate section returns to panels referencing Darboven's early work and artists' postcards, before finally reaching the "index," which lays out the structure of the work and lists *Kulturgeschichte*'s objects.[3]

Newman's description is thorough and economical. Yet as in all descriptions of the work (and even in the most thorough book-length studies, such as Dan Adler's study of the work published in Afterall's One Work series), there is an unmediated telescoping between the presentation of unruly details and the manner in which they precariously hang together as a whole. This summarizes the necessarily synecdochic and truncated character of every attempt to describe it. While this may be the case for any material or visually complex phenomenon, it seems particularly relevant to Darboven's works as they throw viewers back on an emphatic relationship to particularity. What I'm thinking of here is the insistence of the material and graphic artifacts' somewhat awkward irreducibility to the systematic accounting that would subsume them wholly into a general scheme of placement. This difficulty with description is one in which part/whole relations are troubled by what they must elide, what they push to the margins. Darboven's work has been described as "encyclopedic," as an archive, as a collection—all of which are doubtlessly good and true descriptions in terms of historical models of organization and the kinds of subjects and epistemic forms they imply. What they all share, when called to mind in confrontation with the experience of viewing the work, is that they are forms of delimitation and inclusion that imply or promise positive completion—at least rhetorically. This is a moment that Darboven rigorously forecloses, pushing secure descriptive resources out with it.

The trouble with description is worth sticking with for a moment. I've come to think of it as a material feature of much of Darboven's work. The trouble—at least in my experience—is what catalyzes the sometimes inert, utterly finished quality of much of the work. It is a *material effect* that issues from the work's structure and acts as a kind of stave against systemic closure. As Darboven noted: "With me a language is no longer pictorial, it's really structure." Structure is a kind of fact of inscription. It gives rise neither to mental pictures nor any other kind of graphic resemblance. It is non-mimetic and real. I am reminded here of Louis Althusser's Spinozist understanding of structure's absent cause. On this account, causation is understood as a cumulative and combinatory processing of effects: "the structure is immanent in its effects," Althusser writes, "that the whole existence of the structure consists of its effects, in short that the structure, which is merely a specific combination of its peculiar elements, is nothing outside its effects."[4] Effects fold back into structure as a determining ensemble. Structural consistency emerges at the point of a retrojected accumulation of effects. As goes Virgil's maxim, "Add little to little, and there will have emerged a great heap."

This trouble with describing might even be something like a high-level reproduction of Darboven's own rationale, beginning in 1968, for using numerical sequences as well as her later deployment of her agrammatical, yet absolutely ordered cursive scrawl. This rationale almost reaches the level of an injunction in her statement: "I write, but I describe nothing," which is translated from the German "Ich schreibe, aber Ich beschreibe nichts." The threads of translation that are woven throughout Darboven's work illuminate the ban on description. Her maxim (to write without description) is itself the result of a translation of sorts from some advice given—presumably in English—in the 1960s by Carl Andre when she was living in New York: "Never apologize and never explain." (This itself was appropriated from Benjamin Disraeli's aristocratic maxim: "Never complain and never explain.") What is gained of course in the transposition from the English to German is the semantic proximity of the verb *schreiben*—to write—to the verb to describe—*be-schreiben*. Yet a new resonance emerges with the translation of Darboven's internalization of Andre's proscription of explanation *back* into English, where "never explain" re-emerges as "describe nothing." To describe nothing can be taken to signify not only an internalized taboo, but a positive program where "nothing" is taken as a void in need of linguistic circumscription of some sort. (This would seem to fit the notion of the absent cause of structure, positively or materially determined by the effects of a descriptive deficit.) What else would a full transcription of the dates of the century in works such as *Ein Jahrhundert* (*One Century*, 1970–71) be but a way of throwing into relief the materiality of writing as a kind of graphic handle on empty, homogeneous time, simply plodding on in the absence of fulfillment or apocalyptic disruption?

Yet that prematurely solves the problem. Ultimately, to place a finite value on "nothing" as a positive figuration is unsatisfying as a kind of stabilizing trick with language. I don't have an issue with tricks with language; it's the stability part I don't like. Perhaps more compellingly, *de-scription* might be dumbly taken to mean—to negate the scribe, to write out *der Schreiber* (the clerk, typist, or copyist) and thereby cease the task of *in-scription*. This would be something like symbolic death for someone like Darboven, whose life project was to record and reconfigure possibilities for expressing the movement of time as writing.

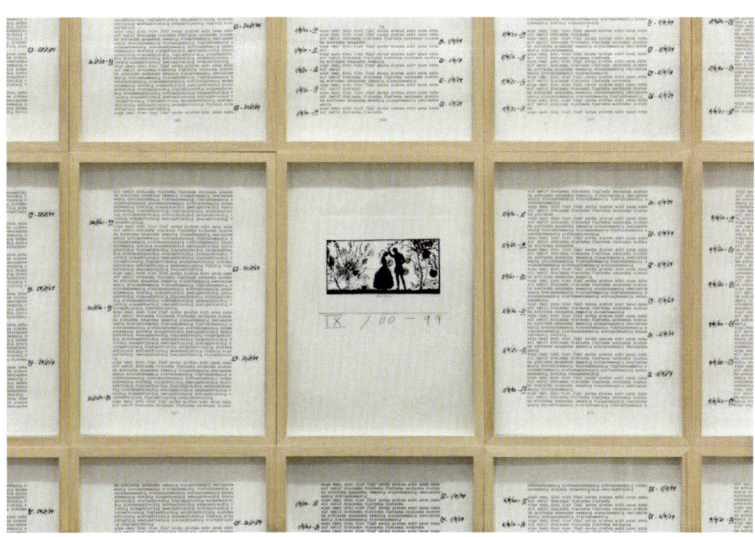

Ein Jahrhundert–Johann Wolfgang von Goethe gewidmet (*One Century–Dedicated to Johann Wolfgang von Goethe*), 1971–82

An intimation of this danger is present in Darboven's statement reported by Lucy Lippard, that "Going on is the enormous thing that I do."[5] Echoed here is the existential dilemma transmitted by the final utterance of the narrator of Samuel Beckett's 1953 novel *The Unnamable*: "You must go on. I can't go on. I'll go on." Going on requires safeguards against description in Darboven's world. Numbering systems are one way in which she sees herself avoiding this danger. Again, quoted by Lippard: "I only use numbers because it is a way of writing without describing. . . . It has nothing to do with mathematics. Nothing! . . . The only thing that has ever been created is the number. A number of something (two chairs, or whatever) is something else. It's not pure number and has other meanings."[6] This is one way in which Darboven's project differentiates itself from the linguistic reductions of a certain analytical model of Conceptual art—and the reference to Joseph Kosuth's chairs is unmistakable.[7] Numbering systems, like Darboven's grammarless cursive script, bind the structure of her works not to the conventions of language understood as a system of meanings, or definitions, or possible statements about the world, but to the graphic structure of its presentation *as writing*. What she jettisons is the possibility of naming a stable or anchoring reference that predicates the writing as a purposeful activity outside of the writer's self-legislating decision "to go on."

The enormity of the task that the writer sets for herself is something like a test of the degree to which decision conditions the way things seem to hang together. She materially fabricates a world for herself out of the materials through which that world comes to be known and signified as continuous, something with internal consistency. If this seems to figure Darboven's labor on the model of an essentially idealist self-constituting subjectivity, then we need only ask what kind of work her writing is. What kind of labor does it recall? Brigid Doherty positions Darboven's labor of going-on within the specific context of the discourse network circa 1900, which Friedrich Kittler formulates in terms of the "flight of ideas" from writing into sheer technical reproduction, associated with the media of gramophone, film, and typewriter. Doherty associates Darboven's writing with a clerical class of women who joined the workforce during the fin de siècle period to perform tasks such as transcribing commercial, bureaucratic, scientific, and cultural information. The early twentieth century feminization of clerical labor mechanized writing as transcription, evacuating the authoritative subject who records sovereign words into the subjectless agency that is transmitted by technical media. Darboven's going-on allows subjectivity to drop out at the same time that it is constituted. She yields the space of the page to the structure of the clerical template. She situates agency as a transcription of historical possibility for inscription. This is a more complex notion of agency than that of the self-identical autonomy of the individual. Agency is like a local thickening of the historical forms that are reproduced in her practical activity of writing. Doherty writes:

> [Darboven's] mathematical prose represents acts of counting and their inscription as phenomena of an experience of the identity of a person mediated by writing, in a sense an identity invented in writing: "my invention—mathematical prose." As Darboven explains, "the transposition of form we call 'content' into an experienced form is very intense. I rewrote by hand in order to be mediated myself by the mediated experience."[8]

If Darboven is written into the scene as an agent of self-conscious mediation, this is as much attributable to copying and calculating as it is to placing strict limits on what can be written and when. Limitation reverberates in the inscriptions one encounters on the first two pages of works such as *Evolution Leibniz* (1986): "and no more words/a day's accounting/and still one world," followed by: "No comment." I can't help but think of another type of clerk, of Herman Melville's Bartleby, in the assertion of "no more words" and the marking of the labor of daily accountings. Darboven's writings form a kind of antipode to Bartleby's suspension of an extraordinary and unflagging capacity to write—or to be exact, to copy—an activity that Darboven is much caught up with in works such as the full transcriptions of entire entries from the Brockhaus Encyclopedia, the *Odyssey*, or in her work *Bismarckzeit* (*Age of Bismarck*, 1978), which includes an incredible array of transcribed source material. In Melville's story, Bartleby dies of self-starvation because his employment as a copyist is the labor that links the graphic reproduction of the law to organic reproduction, and thus to social reproduction. The cessation of one is the death of the other; the cessation of writing is the death of the organism. (Note the image from *Evolution Leibniz* of a toy representing a metalsmith next to a toilet, which is reproduced in the work over and over again. This is simple reproduction in the form of the laboring body as the basic atom of the metabolism of social reproduction.) Unlike Bartleby, Darboven goes on writing, and is extremely clear and explicit about its link to reproduction. She says: "For in the end we all—even I—live by eating, drinking, sleeping. Those are the fundamental truths, but one has to pay for them. I've worked a lot. From this point of view, I don't wish to deny the success of my works."[9] "From this point of view" is a strange locution in this context. The point of view is that of having worked a lot, which is the criterion for the work's success. It is a highly economistic criterion. The time of work is here merely quantified as abstract labor without any other determination. It is work to sustain self-reproduction, often resulting in works whose major operation is the processing of graphic conventions used to quantify the time that it is measured in. This intensely Protestant sentiment would be mundane if not for the utter radicality with which its principle is carried through. Bartlebey's preference to cease reproducing the letter of the law consigns him to nonreproduction, while Darboven's insistence on "going on"

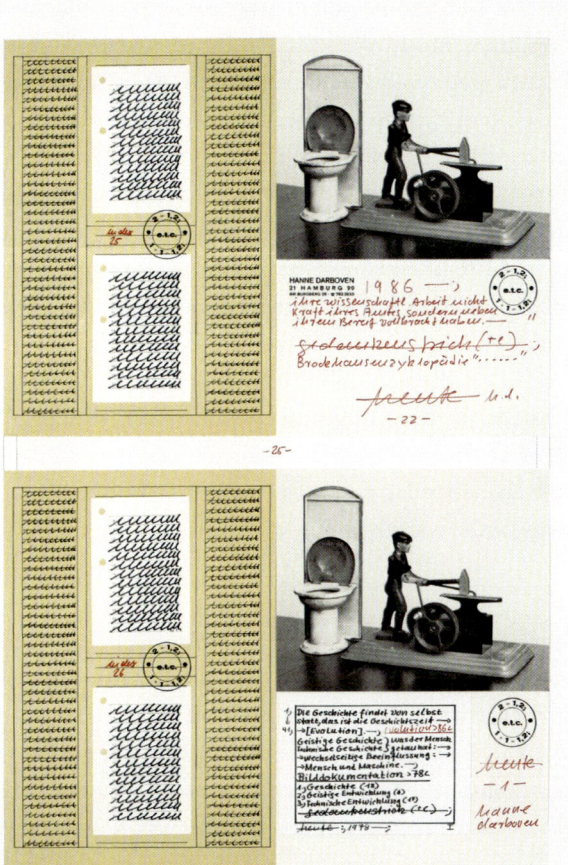

Evolution Leibniz, 1986

reproduces the ceaseless compulsion to make the decision. Her calendrical system, for instance, throws into relief nothing but her own power to write, her own labor power, withdrawing from any other external force of legislation than the preference to "go on" writing.

With her cursive script, she does this by raising to the level of a life project the reproduction of the kinds of inscriptions that one produces precisely when one is not working. Ultimately the antipodes meet—never in the mild middle, always at the extremes. That the necessities of life *must* be paid for here takes on a meaning beyond the hateful middle-class attitude of "facing the facts and getting a job." Both Melville's Bartleby and Darboven *pay for work with their lives*: he by halting the work of writing and thereby perishing; she by making writing the mediating condition of possibility all the way down the line, allowing the agency of writing to overtake the subjectivity of the writer.

III

I want to return to the scene of entering *Cutural History*, or rather the experience of the trouble of entering its mass of visual information. This trouble is enacted in a leap from the work's sheer quantity of information, to a very specific, determined quality. The quality that I'm thinking of must be what it is like to be standing in a net, the gridded mesh of which expands into peripheral vision, stained with shifting rectilinear patterns of graphic details and abrupt shifts of ordering. In other words, I recall the immediate feeling that the work resists any attempt to be read from the *outside*, but rather places viewers in the position of searching for patterns of consistency that would essentially require remaking the work to understand any real fine-grain detail of the internal structure.

In an essay written for Dia's first presentation of *Cultural History* at Dia Center for the Arts, New York, Lynne Cooke notes the resistance

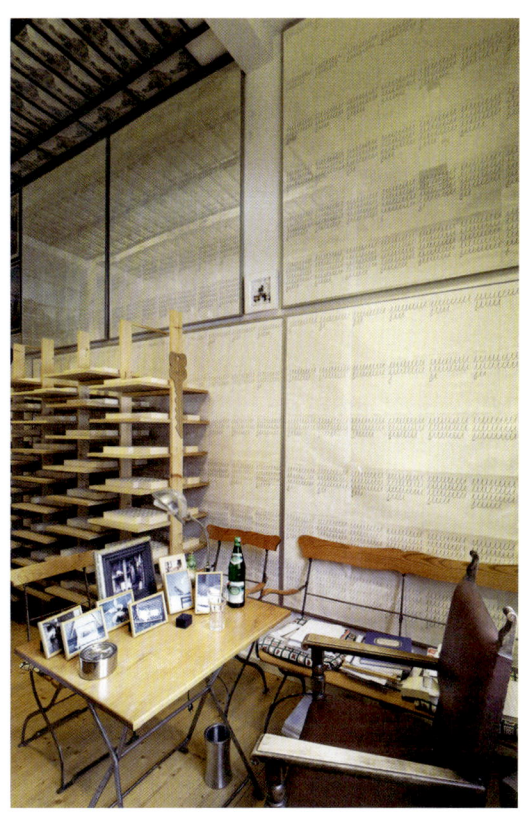

Winter garden desk, Am Burgberg, 2013. Detail: *Ein Jahrhundert–ABC* (*One Century–ABC*), 1970–71

to any overriding systematic interpretive logic that organizes its material. Similarly, Adler notes that the work refuses "to answer the call for interpretive synthesis."[10] This has the effect of dropping viewers into a nonhierarchical mass of historical detail, which collapses the possibility of using any one of its objects or groups of images as an interpretive standpoint. It seems to me that the crucial moment here is the work's ability to augment the intuition of a systematic structure and synthetic standpoint—even if it is empirically absent. This intuition corresponds to an almost paranoid sense that processes of systematic accounting are somehow taking place, independently of any spectatorial will or capacity to locate the lynchpin or key to the work. The lack of a transparent key raises the question of systematicity, settling in either a promise or threat of a closure to the circuitry of its contents. The system is negatively figured in *Cultural History* by virtue of those strange moments in the work where numerical operations and lists become truncated and discontinuous. For instance, in the section of the work containing the Colmer photographs of Manhattan doorways "roman numerals and numbers [which are inscribed] in the corner of each frame indicate that they are meant to be viewed from top to bottom as vertical columns on the wall, but the sequence ends abruptly before reaching the bottom of one row, and switches to an entirely different kind of imagery."[11] These moments allow the elements of the work to upset the logic that is undoubtedly one of its organizational features. In other words, part of the force of a work like *Cultural History* is the maintenance and frustration of this sense of systematic rigor. It simultaneously suspends the possibility and articulates the absence of final closure—of a final description. There is no point at which the net can be pulled closed from the inside, because searching for the handles would undoubtedly involve becoming hopelessly tangled up in the process.

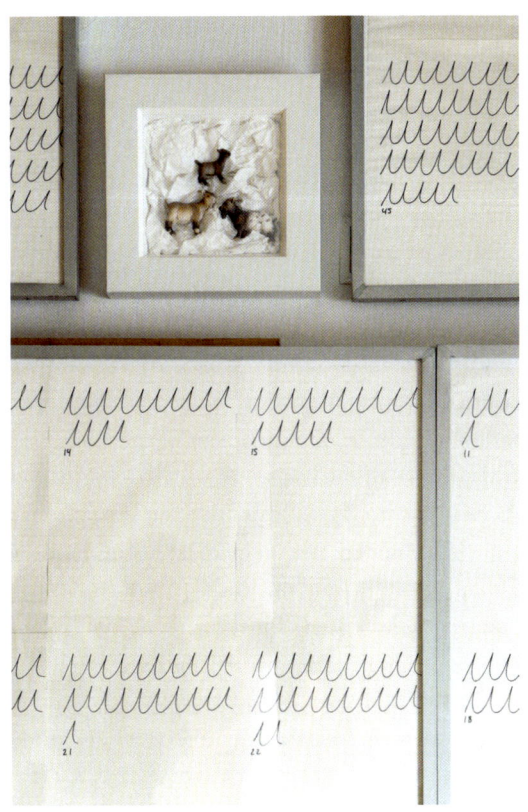

One Century–ABC, 1970–71

I take this figure of the net from Walter Benjamin's 1921 fragment "Capitalism as Religion." In this series of gnomic notes, Benjamin wants to argue that capitalism answers to the same "worries, anguish and disquiet" that religion formerly had.[12] However, regarding the provision of definitive proof of this, he writes: "We cannot draw close the net in which we stand. A commanding overview will, however, later become possible."[13] When this "later" might occur is never answered for in the fragment, nor is it clear under what political or epistemic conditions the overview might arrive. But I think the assertion is not unrelated to what interests me in Darboven's presentation of something like an impossible or self-contradicting overview. The work's title itself—*Cultural History 1880–1983*—might be taken as a performative contradiction, with its strangely isolated, factual presentation as a determining element of the work. Indeed, it names the central concept of the historicist methodology developed by Karl Lamprecht in the fin de siècle period, and is probably better translated as something like "universal cultural history" or "history of civilization" than the literal and misleading "cultural history." Lamprecht's principal thesis stated that the presentation of historical research attains scientific status not through focused reconstruction of empirically exact historical details, but rather through the construction of a general and philosophical synthesis of historical disciplines as well as popular and institutional practices. The synthesis arises from the comparative study of collective psychologies in given periods of time. This is of course in direct contradiction to Darboven's serial—and thus structurally incomplete—and manifestly sensitive—yet psychologically evacuated—relation to detail: quite different from the grubby fingers of historicism groping for totality. Darboven is in the business of severely deferring the position of mastery that wants to subsume seemingly inchoate aggregates of detail under overarching conceptual structures. This is simply a way of saying that the material brought under the purview of systematic conceptualization is weirdly resistant to being either aesthetically or conceptually composed into a picture of totality. The details seem to be continually striking out of a system that thinks it has brought them to order.

Regarding her employment of systematic structures in the late 1960s, Darboven writes: "A system became necessary: how else could I in a concentrated way find something of interest which lends itself to continuation? My systems . . . work in terms of progressions and/or reductions. . . . In this moment I know about what I did. What I am doing, what will happen further, I shall see."[14] "I shall see" faintly echoes Benjamin's "commanding overview [that] will . . . later become possible." To reach the bottom line, to finally balance the accounts, would be nothing short of perilous for the functionality of those concepts as regulating principles—debt, in the end, does not want to be satisfied. Its relief continually recedes from the vantage point that has been entirely organized and principled by it.

I think the context of Benjamin's fragment is not coincidental to Darboven's barring of a final synthetic moment of understanding or completion. One of Benjamin's claims is that the development of capitalism supplanted transcendent, religious authority with the unending cult of economic calculation. The dates of *Cultural History 1880–1983* are firmly grounded (if perhaps arbitrarily designated) within the development and regression of capitalist forces of subjection to the cult. The notion of final synthetic adequation—whether of Spirit or the bottom line—has an old and very Germanic history. It culminates in a history of thought that wants to understand the equation of both logical and historical theories of synthesis with monetary and economic ones. This finds its highest elaboration in the nineteenth-century philosopher Hegel and his account of the theodicy of Spirit through the painful machinations of successive sublations of rationality and history. Sublation (*Aufhebung*) is the movement of simultaneous cancellation and transcendence of the concept in time (Hegel: "Philosophy is time comprehended in thought"). This double movement of the concept in its path to self-consciousness has a uniquely monetary origin in the language that serves as its basis. Marc Shell writes that:

> In its initial stages Hegel's intellectual method [sublation] is similar to the arithmetic one of contemporary German accountants. In German states in the eighteenth century, most merchants did their accounts by manipulating tallies or checkers on a board. (In Hegel's time the English Chancellor of the Exchequer still used this method. . . .) In reckoning, "the tallies of counters used for working out problems on a board were 'picked-up [*aufgehobene*]' when dealt with; thus if one was picked-up from either side, the result that remained was unaffected." The money token, or checker, was cancelled without changing the total. The cancellation of the opposing part became a partial means toward indicating the one whole.

> The historical transition from reckoning with this checkerboard to figuring with Arabic numerals, algorithm, and the sign for naught (the cipher "0") was a significant turning point in western thought. The new "algebra" of double-entry bookkeeping had been "discovered" by 9th century Arabs who needed an efficient method to calculate inheritance shares. Their discovery influenced analysis of simple and dialectical opposition.[15]

The association of double-entry bookkeeping as a procedure inflatable to the heights of philosophical thought prioritizes equation and adequation to zero. First one brings the negative term of an equation up to a positive value through addition on one side of the account book, thus allowing a new figure to emerge from negation; a process which is repeated on the other side of the equation by confronting similar and congruent terms and eliminating them. Darboven's mathematical prose directly deploys the formats involved in this kind of processing of accounts. Yet she asserts a concrete scheme of accumulation that makes her reckoning of the numbers irreducible to the synthesis of sums into balanced accounts—distancing her work

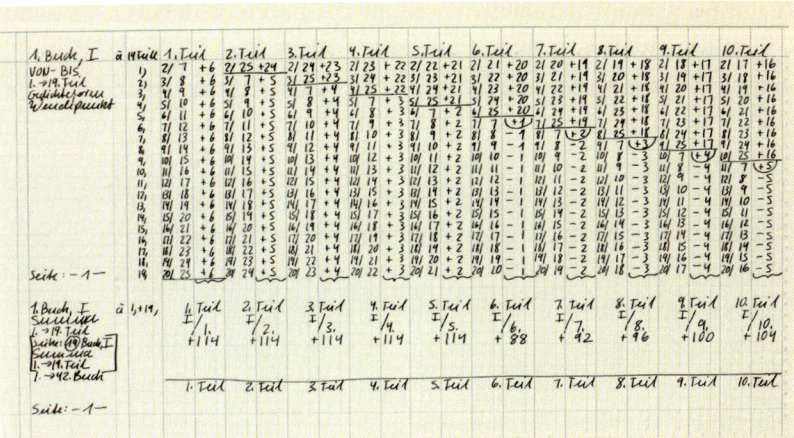

Requiem, Opus 19, I. Buch (Requiem, Opus 19, Book I), 1985–88

at the same time from the algorithmic foundations of all manner of computation into the present. "My work surely isn't incomprehensible manipulation of data in the sense of our computer age," she says in an interview, "but rather starts with 2 = 1,2. We all depend on this simple mathematical system, whether we're buying ourselves a loaf of bread or the power of the atom bomb is being measured.[16] *Cultural History* implies this accumulative scheme as a background to her double-page spreads on which the accounts of modernity seem to keep piling up. She renounces the reduction to "0" not only as a logical starting point, but also as a graphic effect. The work weaves the net from the aging detritus of a forestalled synthetic overview.

From this position, the work resonates less with Hegel and more with Friedrich Schlegel, who, with the full force of Romantic irony, writes: "It is equally as fatal to have a system as not to have one." This is a double bind rather than double bookkeeping. The bind is as painful as they come, or perhaps as comical as it gets. (Who can decide?) It coaxes the kind of thought that only the best sort of fatalism has to impart. Namely, that postulating a systematic *overview* runs the risk of liquidating the particulars that gain in intelligibility through the relationships facilitated by that subsumption. But the insight runs deeper than an ironic observation on the effects that system building has on the one who came up with it, that "has" it. The insight goes right down to a moment of inversion, where who or what "has" the system is thrown into doubt. And I relate this to Darboven's role as an agent that is as much constituted as crossed out by her work. The possession of a system of thought or praxis collapses into the fatal attraction that the system has to its own logic. Every system is in the business of having to continually catch itself, to violently consummate possession of what is not it. Every systematic attempt to manage the crisis of incoherence and contingency is sublimated and reproduced as the crisis *of* the system, in the same

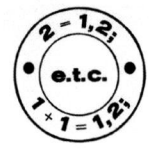

sense that Theodor W. Adorno writes that a constant antagonism forms part of the concept of totality. The principle of totality sets limits on itself, even if it only be in the commandment to resemble itself—to subsume all of its moments under the same identifying force, which has to be continually reinforced and corrected in the behavior of its subjects.

Darboven writes something *out* of the system—in the sense of both emerging from it and becoming unaccountable to it. The possibility for description, self-assured subjective placement, the frustration of an overview: it is only from the vantage point of an element, looking back from elsewhere, that the system can be seen in its totality as something finite, contingent, and ripped apart by its own antagonistic form. This vantage point is never attained, but is thinkable as a commanding overview not yet written.

ECLIPSE . . .

The earth wanders like any other planet. It hurtles through space, wheeling around its axis as, in company with other planets, it circles the sun. The terrestrial terrain is by no means cosmically unique, except for the fact that, as far as we know, it is the only planet with inhabitants so utterly in the thrall of their own image. Less than twenty years before the termination date of Darboven's *Cultural History*, in August 1966, *Lunar Orbiter I* sent back the first images of the earth, emerging from the shadow of the moon.

Three years later marked the date of the first lunar landing. The historical philosopher Hans Blumenberg saw in this event the dislocation implied in the capacity to picture the whole. The Copernican world is decentered by its image. He wrote: "[P]erhaps it would not have been necessary to send people to the Moon at all if what was to be brought back was, above all, pictures."[17] To depict the earth as a whole, as

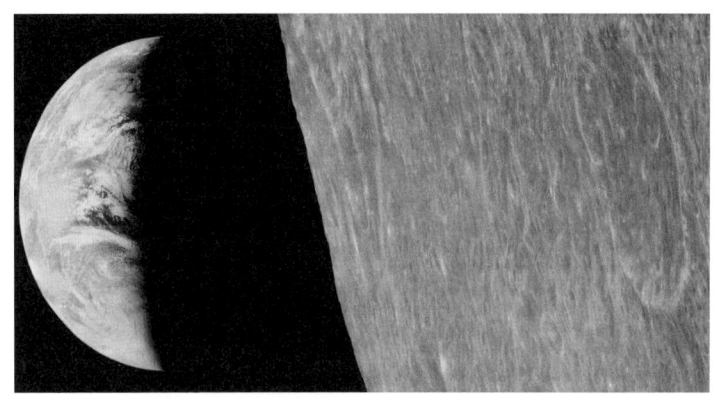

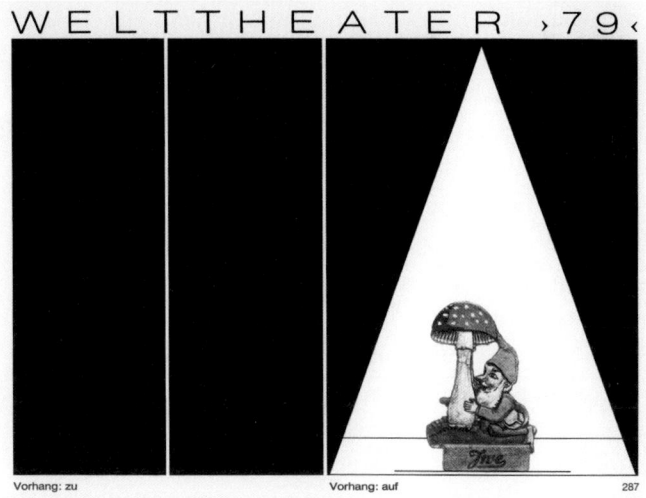

Vorhang: zu

Vorhang: auf

287

Earthrise, 1966
Welttheater 79, 1979

a complete sphere in a proliferation of technically reproduced images, was to allow that wholeness to emerge by virtue of assuming another standpoint: that of the moon, which allows light to filter in from elsewhere.

It is only at this point that the Elizabethan dream of the world theater is actualized. Writing (in this case: writing in light) is its stage management. But the script keeps rehearsing unresolved conflicts that countermand the idyllic image of the earth from space—whether we are talking about the bone-crushing wheels of Saint-Aubin's drawings, orbiting behind the scenes of the unmaintainable humanistic ornamentation of eighteenth-century clerks' offices; or the mass of data held in server space, whose overheating cores threaten to melt into the magma of an uninhabitable frozen wasteland. The system *is* the crisis that afflicts it, as the slogan runs. The more information that piles in, the more legibility is filtered out, requiring new measures of processing that displace anything like a human reader.

If in the 1960s the counterculture was reading the *Whole Earth Catalog*, ensnared by its optimism for a newfound, earthbound system-imminence, Darboven's counter-*Kultur* cataloguing might be said to look back at the place from which the overview makes its claim on totality. From within the mesh of world, the limits of the globe seem to be more conditioning and urgent than ever.

The moon is cast into crescent form by the shadow of the world, providing access to the image of a closed sphere.

The negative space of the crescent is knocked out and reproduced as a cheap trinket placed in the ear of a mannequin in the image of a child—its smile resolving into its own crescent grimace, surrounded by accumulated fragments, each of which deny the closure they cumulatively seem to indicate.

"And no more words/a day's accounting/and still one world"— "No comment."

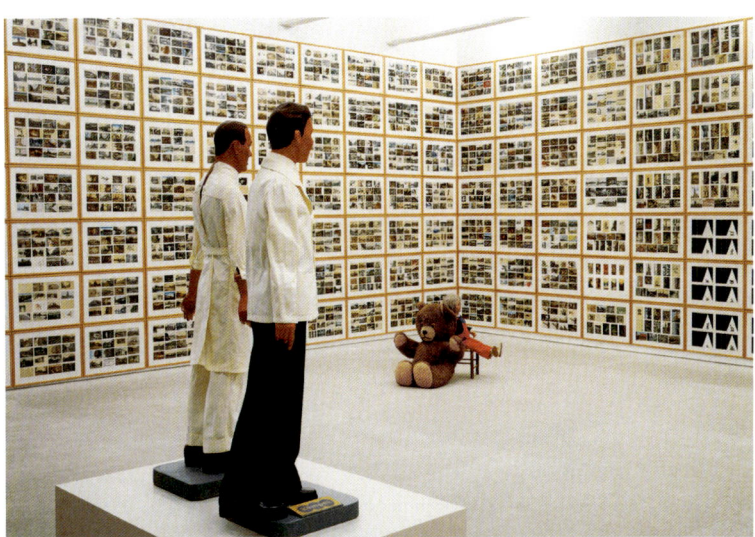

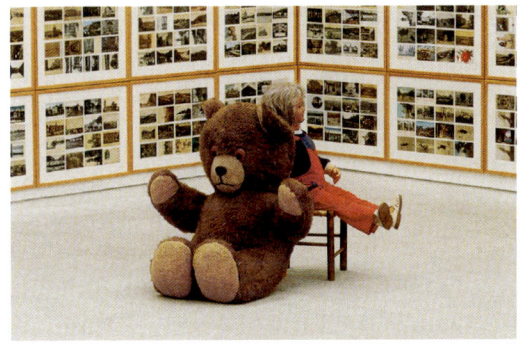

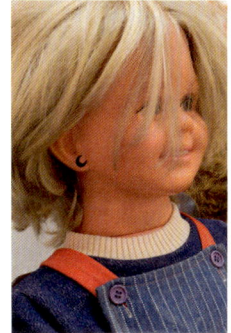

Cultural History 1880–1983. Dia Center for the Arts, New York, 1996–97

notes

Epigraph: Monique Wittig, *Les Guérillères*, trans. David LeVay (Urbana: University of Illinois Press, 2007), p. 97.

1 Ben Kafka, *The Demon of Writing: Powers and Failures of Paperwork* (New York: Zone Books, 2012), p. 22.

2 Ibid.

3 Michael Newman, "Remembering and Repeating: Hanne Darboven's Work," in *Robert Lehman Lectures on Contemporary Art*, ed. Lynne Cooke and Karen Kelly, vol. 2 (New York: Dia Art Foundation, 2004), pp. 123–25.

4 Louis Althusser and Étienne Balibar, *Reading Capital*, trans. Ben Brewster (London: New Left Books, 1970), p. 189.

5 Lucy Lippard, "Hanne Darboven: Deep in Numbers," *Artforum* 12, no. 2 (October 1973), p. 37.

6 Lippard, "Hanne Darboven: Deep in Numbers," pp. 35–36.

7 Joseph Kosuth created *One and Three Chairs* in 1965.

8 Brigid Doherty, "Hanne Darboven's 'Real Writing' of History," *Hanne Darboven: Menschen und Landshaften*, ed. Kira van Lil (Hamburg: Christians, 1999), pp. 39–40; for Friedrich Kittler, see also Kittler, *Discourse Networks 1800/1900*, trans. Michael Metteer, with Chris Cullens (Stanford: Stanford University Press, 1990).

9 Darboven, quoted in Dan Adler, *Hanne Darboven: Cultural History 1880–1983* (London: Afterall Books, 2009), p. 106, n. 80.

10 Lynne Cooke, "*Hanne Darboven: Kulturgeschichte 1880–1983*, 1980–83," exhibition brochure (New York: Dia Art Foundation, 1996), n.p.; Adler, *Hanne Darboven*, p. 4.

11 Adler, *Hanne Darboven*, p. 5.

12 Walter Benjamin, "Capitalism as Religion" (1921), trans. Chad Kautzer, in *The Frankfurt School on Religion: Key Writings by the Major Thinkers*, ed. Eduardo Mendieta (New York: Routledge, 2005), p. 259.

13 Ibid.

14 Hanne Darboven, "Artists on Art," *Art International* 12, no. 4 (April 20, 1968), p. 55.

15 Marc Shell, *Money, Language, and Thought: Literary and Philosophical Economies from the Medieval to the Modern Era* (University of California, 1982; Baltimore: Johns Hopkins University Press, 1993), p. 142.

16 Darboven, in *Hanne Darboven: Primitive Zeit/Uhrzeit* (*Primitive Time/Clock Time*), exh. cat. (Philadelphia: Goldie Paley Gallery, Moore College of Art and Design, 1991), p. 15.

17 Hans Blumenberg, *The Genesis of the Copernican World*, trans. Robert N. Wallace (Cambridge, Mass.: MIT Press, 1987), p. 676.

Sam Lewitt's lecture on Hanne Darboven took place at Dia:Chelsea, New York, on December 16, 2014.

Josephine Meckseper
War and Object

1997 was the year when I first saw a major exhibition of Hanne Darboven's work. *Kulturgeschichte 1880–1983 (Cultural History 1880–1983*, 1980–83) was installed at Dia Center for the Arts in New York. I remember being struck by its radical, conceptual, all-encompassing nature and the numerous historical and political references to Darboven's own life that could be traced through these works. There are images that relate to her having been raised near Hamburg during World War II, coming to New York during the politically charged Vietnam War era, and witnessing the revolts of 1968 in Germany, as well as the subsequent Cold War decades. It was also around the same time that I saw Gerhard Richter's complete *Atlas* (1962–) at documenta 10 in Kassel. Both bodies of work moved me, in the ways in which they dealt with the imagery and trauma of Germany's war crimes and genocides, and the weight of the twentieth century as a whole.

   Darboven specifically confronts the notion of Enlightenment in Europe, specifically Germany, with the regressive and catastrophic nature of fascism. The overarching theme of Enlightenment and encyclopedic historical accumulation is an important note in relationship to Darboven's work, in which she frequently references key Enlightenment figures like Johann Wolfgang von Goethe and Gottfried Wilhelm Leibnitz. The *Encyclopédie* published by Denis Diderot and Jean le Rond d'Alembert in France between 1751 and 1772 is a first manifestation of how the idea of Enlightenment could be put together in a humanistic encyclopedia that based its entire

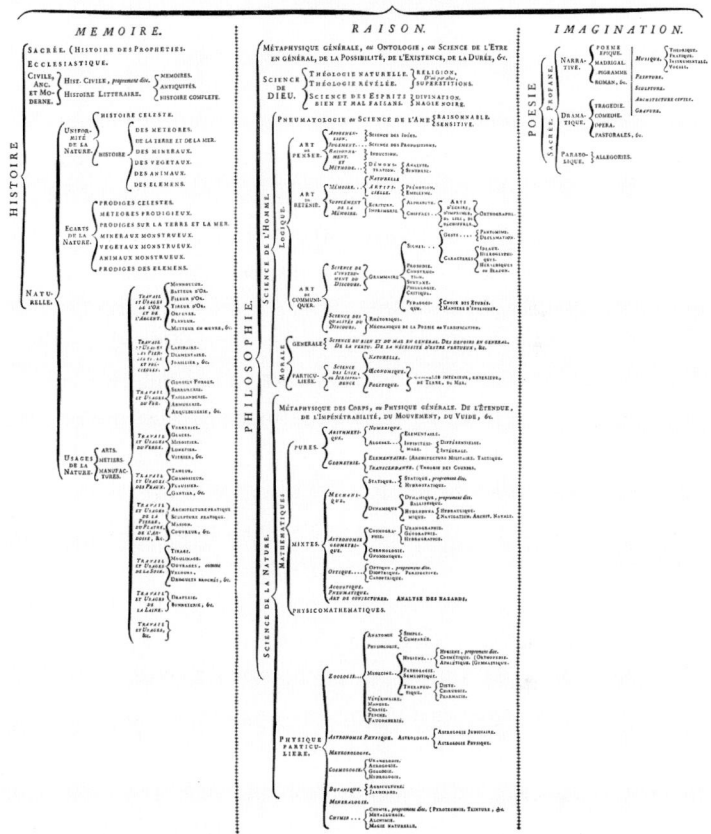

"Système figuré des connoissances humaines," from *Encyclopédie*, 1751

system on the idea of memory, reason, and imagination.[1] It contained 71,818 articles and 3,129 illustrations in 35 volumes.

Otto von Bismarck, the minister president of Prussia from 1862 to 1890 who oversaw the unification of Germany, also played an important role in Darboven's work. She centered her 1978 project *Bismarckzeit* (*Age of Bismarck*) around his persona, and his bust is one of the nineteen sculptural components of *Cultural History*. Historically he symbolizes the era that ended the Enlightenment and led Europe into World War I and World War II. Within her work, Darboven investigates a relationship between art and history, and she contrasts Bismarck's un-ideological real politics with Hitler's irrational catastrophic politics of destruction.[2]

Darboven was in many ways influenced by the writing of Theodor W. Adorno, a leading member of the Frankfurt School. Adorno had been expelled from his teaching position in Germany because of his Jewish heritage. While exiled in California during World War II, he developed a critical theory of what he termed the culture industry. The sameness he saw in movies, radio, and magazines reminded him of the standardized production of a factory, and the passivity these formats required of their consumers struck him as authoritarian. He was an outspoken opponent of fascism, and with Max Horkheimer he wrote *Dialectic of Enlightenment* (1947), which traced links between the rise of both mass culture and fascism in the failures of modernism and the Enlightenment. These ideas would be very influential on the European New Left. Darboven clearly had him in mind when she made *Requiem for M. Oppenheimer* (1985), which, among other things, includes musical instruments, or it represents musical instruments, that Jewish musicians in concentration camps would play to entertain their captors. The written wall elements of the work reference Adorno's proposition, "to write poetry after Auschwitz is barbaric."[3]

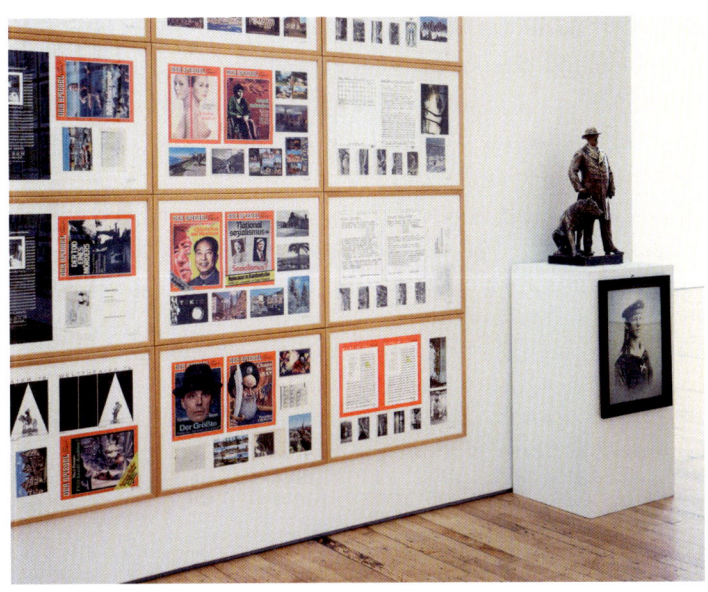

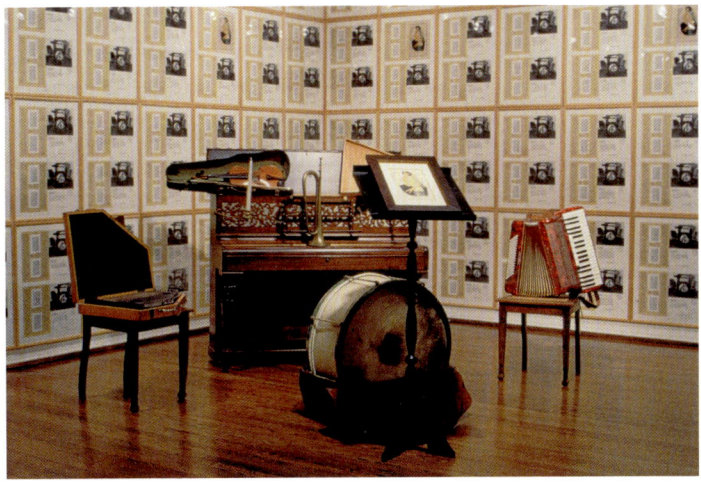

Cultural History 1880–1983, 1980–83. Dia:Beacon, Beacon, New York, 2003
Requiem for M. Oppenheimer, 1985. Leo Castelli Gallery, New York, 1990

In the 1989 documentary *Architecture of Doom*, director Peter Cohen explores how Nazi Germany employed art as an effective conveyor of propaganda and provided cover for genocide and the annexation of neighboring countries. The film shows how art was vastly instrumentalized during that time.

> Germany celebrates German Arts Day in Munich, 1939. It is the Third Reich's last major art exhibit. Within six weeks, the Second World War would commence. "Yes, this government, half of which consists of men who once aspired to serve the arts, is conscious of the artist's role as an intermediary," declares Hans-Friedrich Blunck, author and president of the Reich's Chamber of Literature. He continues, "This government, born out of the opposition to rationalism, knows the people's inner longings, their boundless dreams, to which only the artist can give form."[4]

Art loses its legitimacy as a communicative form in the light of the Nazi atrocities. This is the basis of Darboven's art; her work is engaged in accumulating the leftover parts from the collapse of the Enlightenment. Perhaps, Darboven is suggesting that the historical events of Nazi Germany cannot be rationalized. Instead, they need to be relived and revisited on a daily basis, which she does by writing, cataloging, and collecting evidence of irrationality.

Aside from the installations and books, the core of her work might have been a daily performance of lived information that she executed in her own studio, almost like a ritual.

The found objects and artifacts from her own extensive collection become witnesses and demonstrate how objects are no longer innocent, and that they carry meaning way beyond aesthetic form, after having lived through World War II and the Nazi regime. Michael Newman addressed this in his reflection on *Cultural History*, attributing a "future pastness" to what he described as "second-order found objects, objects that could be described as having been made to be found." He notes, "The most troubling case is not so much the cross,

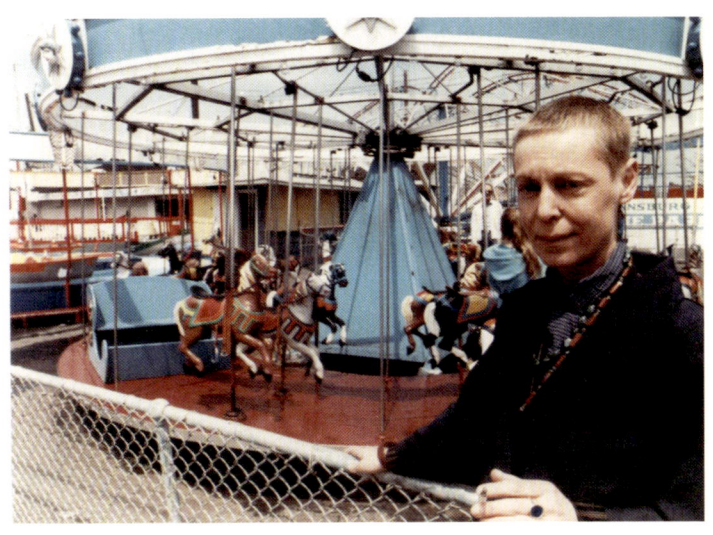

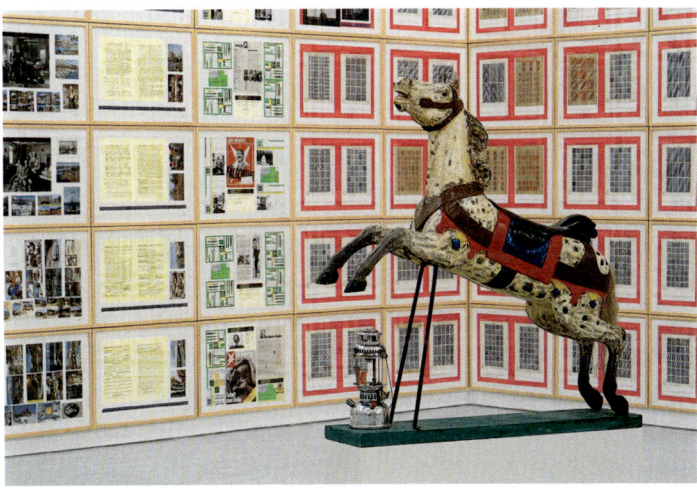

Hanne Darboven in Keansburg, New Jersey, 1989
Cultural History 1880–1983. Dia Center for the Arts, New York, 1996–97

which has disturbed some people, but the emblematic rearing fairground horse with the Chinese-made lamp, which Darboven says represent a warhorse and the gas chambers of World War II death camps."[5] And from what I've found and read, she had entire warehouses filled with these types of found objects and huge collections of writings and pictures.

From early on until her death in 2009, Darboven's home was in a small village near Hamburg called Rönneburg. Hamburg played an important strategic role for the Allied Forces during World War II, because of a massive firebombing on the city in July 1943, when Darboven was two years old. The Darboven family had to flee when a bomb struck near their home; the event was one of the artist's first memories.[6] The Battle of Hamburg, also code-named Operation Gomorrah, was a campaign of air raids for eight days and seven nights. It was at the time the heaviest assault in the history of aerial warfare, and it was later called the Hiroshima of Germany.[7] Operation Gomorrah killed 42,600 people and left 37,000 wounded, and over one million people had to evacuate the city. No subsequent city raid shook Germany more than the one on Hamburg. Not even the one in Dresden came close.

One could argue that the lists and numbers that Darboven compiled in her studio are a haunting reflection on the lists that the genocidal Nazis carried of their victims. The final solution to the Jewish question, established at the Wannsee Conference on January 20, 1942, made this official policy, and Adolf Eichmann drew up lists of Jewish populations in occupied countries. It was Eichmann's meticulous record keeping and bureaucratic distance from the Holocaust he managed that led to Hannah Arendt's observation on the banality of evil.

> The Ministry of Finance and the Reichsbank prepared facilities to receive the huge loot from all over Europe, down to watches and gold teeth, all of which was sorted out in the Reichsbank and then sent to the Prussian

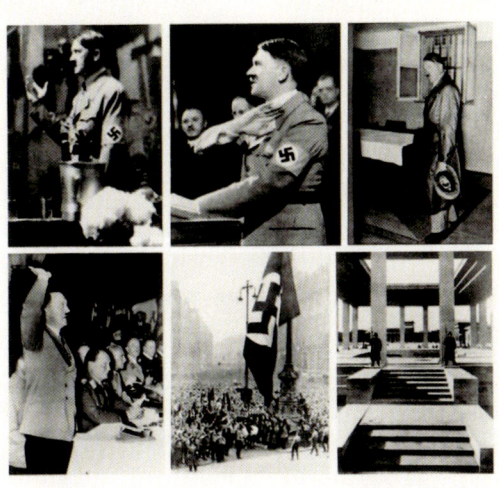

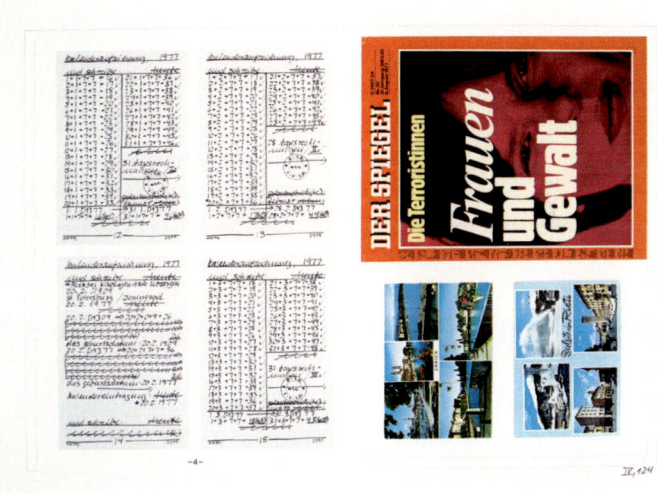

Gerhard Richter, *Atlas*, 1962– . Detail: panel 131
Cultural History 1880–1983. Detail: IV/124

State Mint. The Ministry of Transport provided the necessary railroad cars, usually freight cars, even in times of great scarcity of rolling stock, and they saw to it that the schedule of the deportation trains did not conflict with other timetables. The Jewish Councils of Elders were informed by Eichmann or his men of how many Jews were needed to fill each train, and they made out the list of deportees. The Jews registered, filled out innumerable forms, answered pages and pages of questionnaires regarding their property so that it could be seized the more easily; they then assembled at the collection points and boarded the trains. The few who tried to hide or to escape were rounded up by a special Jewish police force.[8]

While Hitler was committing war crimes of unimaginable dimensions, he also carried out a megalomaniacal personal building project, an alpine construction to serve as his retreat. The narrator of *Architecture of Doom* spoke of Hitler's artistic ambitions for his Bavarian estate:

Hitler decided to rebuild his chalet in Berchtesgaden, to have it befit his new status. To this end, he not only produced sketches, but completely took over the re-planning of Berghof, his retreat. The original house was to be part of the new structure. The result was amateurish. Obvious weaknesses flaw the design: an alpine chalet aspiring to be a chateau. Hitler's pride was a retractable window, the world's biggest, with an area of thirty-two square meters. At Berghof, the monumental is paired with the petit bourgeois in a bizarre way. The world's biggest retractable window is still a chalet window, after all, a bourgeois dream absurdly inflated. The window on the landscape, like the glass over a painting, embodied Hitler's aesthetic ideal. Mountain landscapes were among his favorite motifs. At the Great German Art Exhibit in 1938, Hitler buys not only *Zugspitzmassiv* by Franz Bernhard, but nine other paintings of alpine scenes.

A number of panels in *Cultural History* present similar picture postcards of German mountain scenes. The relationship between Hitler's delusional chalet project and the war crimes he committed simultaneously might have provoked Darboven to pick up on this type of imagery in her time, although the specific postcards that she used

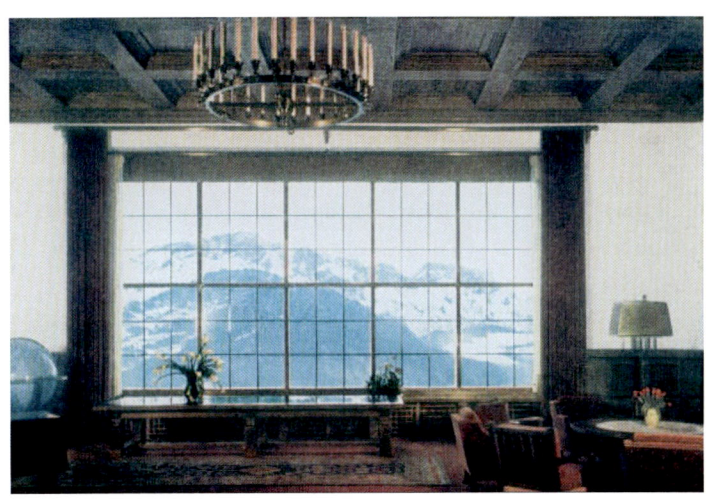

Interior view of a massive window in the Great Room of the Berghof, Adolf Hitler's estate in Berchtesgaden, Upper Bavaria, late 1930s

are decisively from before World War II—almost as if she was trying to unburden them from this association. Still, they show us how the picturesque could never be the same after World War II and the Nazi regime. In its aftermath, we are facing a completely new reality of how to relate to art and authorship.

One could draw a parallel to Roland Barthes's "Death of the Author" in Darboven's work, since she carries out an act of un-performing a collective historical burden through her encyclopedic works liberated from individualistic self-expression. "The author," according to Barthes, "is a modern figure, a product of our society insofar as, emerging from the Middle Ages with English empiricism, French rationalism and the personal faith of the Reformation, it discovered the prestige of the individual, of, as it is more nobly put, the 'human person.'"[9] In the same way Barthes sees in Bertolt Brecht a rupture in the hyper-individualistic artist figure, Darboven exercises a similar principle by creating selfless perspectives through accumulation and detachment. "The removal of the Author (one could talk here with Brecht of a veritable 'distancing', the Author diminishing like a figurine at the far end of the literary stage). . . ."[10]

Richter also picked up on the mountain theme in his *Atlas* project, which he began in 1962. He produced over 780 panels, with more than 4,000 images. They include amateur family snapshots and reproductions from newspapers and popular magazines. Almost every photograph in Richter's *Atlas* project is a carefully managed reproduction, though, in order to create a standardized display that is somewhat comparable to Darboven's. As is the case with her work, Richter's photographic imagery may be read as an act of tracing and distancing from crimes and violent acts committed by Nazi Germany.

He also shares with Darboven the same reaction and approach to the atrocities of the Holocaust and World War II—that it's really

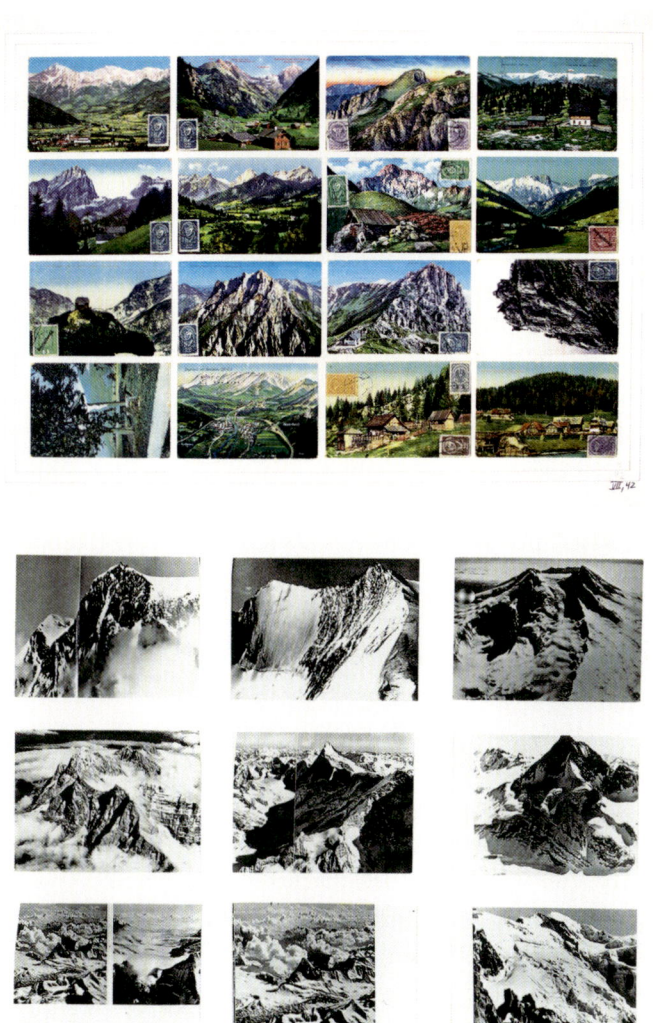

Cultural History 1880–1983. Detail: VII/42

Gerhard Richter, *Atlas*, 1962– . Detail: panel 125

impossible to make sense of and cannot be reconciled. By accumulating and reframing images and documents related to this time, they both point to the fact that the past can never truly be processed; the trauma can never be resolved.

The German newsmagazine *Der Spiegel*'s trademark red frame brackets many of Darboven's works. It could be interpreted as a reference to the Enlightenment, as the magazine represents a leftist political voice that could stand for the idea of the Enlightenment. But it can also be read as a metaphor for reoccurrence and periodicity since it is a weekly publication that Darboven chose in order to demonstrate the repetitive, performative nature of the content that she is putting on display in *Cultural History*. Is she perhaps emphasizing the marking of every day as a way to prevent memories from simply being forgotten in ordinary daily routines?

Horkheimer and Adorno's "Enlightenment as Mass Deception" comes to mind: "Culture today is infecting everything with sameness. . . . Culture is a paradoxical commodity. It is so completely subject to the law of exchange that it is no longer exchanged; it is so blindly equated with use that it can no longer be used. For this reason it merges with the advertisement. The more meaningless the latter appears under monopoly, the more omnipotent culture becomes."[11]

Der Spiegel's headquarters are in Hamburg, near where Darboven had her studio. Hamburg was the city where all the publishing houses were located after World War II. So the fact that she references media, or magazines like *Der Spiegel* or *Stern*, might also have to do with how this was all taking place right around the corner from where she lived. When I moved to New York in the nineties, I worked for *Der Spiegel* for a few years, as a freelance editor. It was around the same time that I saw Darboven's works at Dia.

I grew up not far from Hamburg myself, although almost three decades later than Darboven did. As a teenager, I participated in an antinuclear power demonstrations near Hamburg. My hometown of Worpswede is actually a Utopian artist colony founded at the beginning of the twentieth century, with a rare combination of Jugendstil, German Expressionist, and Modernist architecture, and Rainer Maria Rilke spent several years there.

Throughout the nineties, I published a conceptual magazine called *FAT*. Several artists and writers that I knew from my student years at California Institute of the Arts were involved and contributed to the magazine. The magazine was distributed at regular newsstands, but also exhibited in wallpaper form. It was inspired by political theorist and radical publisher Jean-Paul Marat's newspaper *L'Ami du peuple* from the French Revolution and the avant-gardist tradition of breaking down barriers between art and life. Artworks by artists like Monica Bonvicini, Robert Longo, and Matthew Barney were disguised as advertisements. One issue featured an interview with Dan Graham, who started his career as an artist by presenting work in magazines and who was interested in the ways unrelated magazine content juxtaposed:

> If I were to put something in a magazine, it would interact with the content of that particular issue. In other words, typically every issue had a different thematic content, so there was a relation between one page and another page—and a relationship to the theme, which would be dated when the issue was over. It was important that it just be an insertion. There was the first thing I did in '65 for a magazine, a grocery receipt that didn't add up to anything. So, in one sense it just looked like figures. And, of course, it's next to advertisements.[12]

FAT was both about infiltrating popular culture and subverting the idea of distribution and commerce of art and its reproduction. When in 1999 the Seattle riots broke out, I decided with my collaborators that the magazine principle could morph into a conceptual "shop window"—the icon of consumer culture, target, and collateral damage at any relevant demonstration. The pairing of oppositional voices such as advertising language and protest signage became a crucial factor in the conceptualization of these window installations. I began setting up a relationship between filming the ongoing antiwar and anticapitalist protests in New York and the surrounding urban shop window displays on the streets. The window installations were intended to look like protest "targets" and often included broken mirrors.

This was a continuous train of thought, having grown up in West Germany in the seventies, where a very similar revolt against corporate capitalism and politics was taking place and had an impact on my immediate environment. The imagery and sentiment of the leftist revolts of the seventies, which my family had ties to, had a large influence on my works.

In the seventies and eighties, Darboven's work started showing references to the political unrest of the sixties and seventies, especially the leftist movements and how Germany's Red Army Faction (RAF) was revolting against the presence of Nazis in high-ranked positions in postwar Germany.[13]

Hamburg was also the home of *Konkret*, a monthly German magazine for politics and culture, which was founded in 1957. *Konkret* was a radical left-wing magazine at the time. Ulrike Meinhof served as the editor in chief from 1962 to 1964. After an assassination attempt on a German student activist in 1968, Meinhof wrote a cover article for *Konkret*, "From Protest to Resistance." Echoing Fred Hampton, she argued for the legitimacy of violence in resistance against political power: "Protest is when I say I don't like this and that. Resistance is when I see to it that things that I don't like no longer occur."[14] Soon after, she left the magazine and joined the RAF, which became known as the Baader-Meinhof Group.

The letters and manifestos of the RAF demonstrated extreme opposition to a capitalist system that underwrote violent and

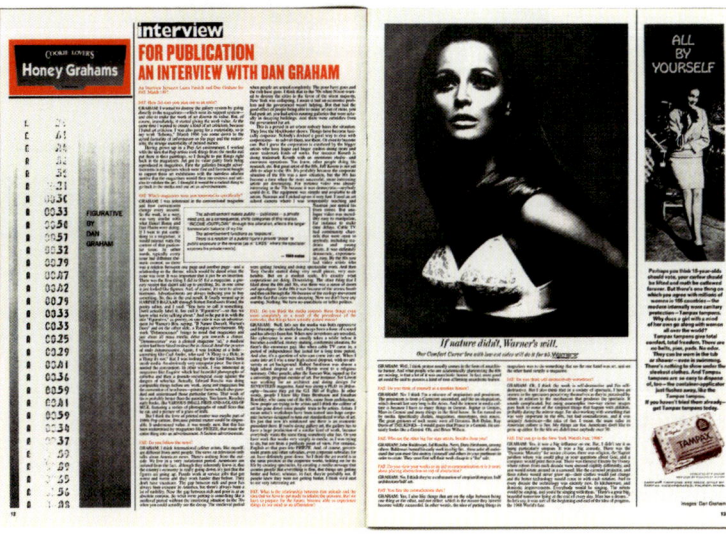

COOKIE LOVERS
Honey Grahams

interview
FOR PUBLICATION
AN INTERVIEW WITH DAN GRAHAM

FIGURATIVE
BY
DAN GRAHAM

If nature didn't, Warner's will.

The Comfort Curve bra with low-cut sides will do it for it. Warner's

ALL
BY
YOURSELF

imperialist acts like the Vietnam War, and instead the group agitated for a communist revolution.

> How can we allow them to murder in our name? Americans, out of Vietnam. We have demonstrated once too often in an orderly, appropriate, and unsuccessful fashion. We have had enough of providing the veneer of democracy.

> In Western society, the system has managed to drag the masses so deeply into their own crap that they seem to have lost any feeling of their position as exploited and oppressed, so that they dream of nothing more than a car, a holiday, and a tiled bathroom.[15]

In a BBC documentary about the Baader-Meinhof Group, *Generation Terror*, this last excerpt is accompanied by footage of department-store shopping displays, racks of sunglasses and televisions and mannequins. The footage reminds me of a particular detail of *Cultural History*, where Darboven dressed a male and female mannequin in training tracksuits. The concept of capitalism and its relationship to the politics of that era are depicted in the panels on the wall behind those mannequins, and they show the issues that the Baader-Meinhof Group was so heavily fighting against. Meinhof used the example of the department store to encapsulate her views on violent resistance: "The progressive aspects of setting fire to a department store do not lie in the destruction of goods, but in the criminal act, in breaking the law. . . . The law that gets broken when department stores are set on fire is not a law that protects people. It is a law that protects property."[16]

There are a few details in *Cultural History* that show images of what Darboven was collecting while she was in New York, between 1966 and 1968. The photographs of Manhattan doorways in her work were not her own; she collaborated, or rather, she asked the photographer Roy Colmer for permission to incorporate his photography in her work. He had started a very extensive process of photographing

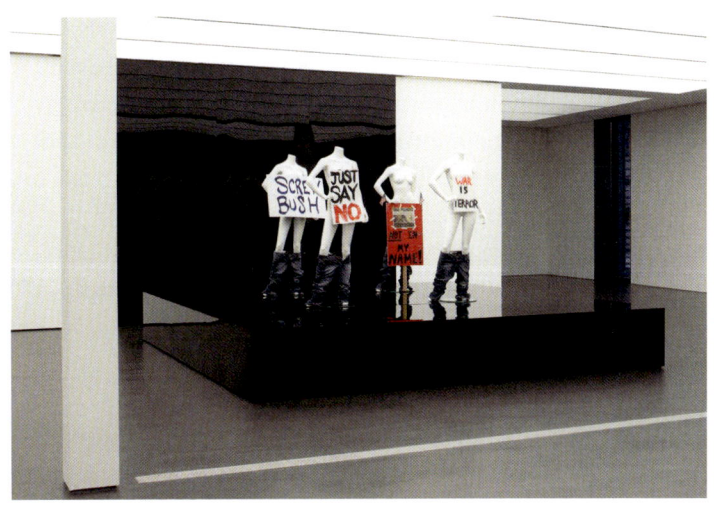

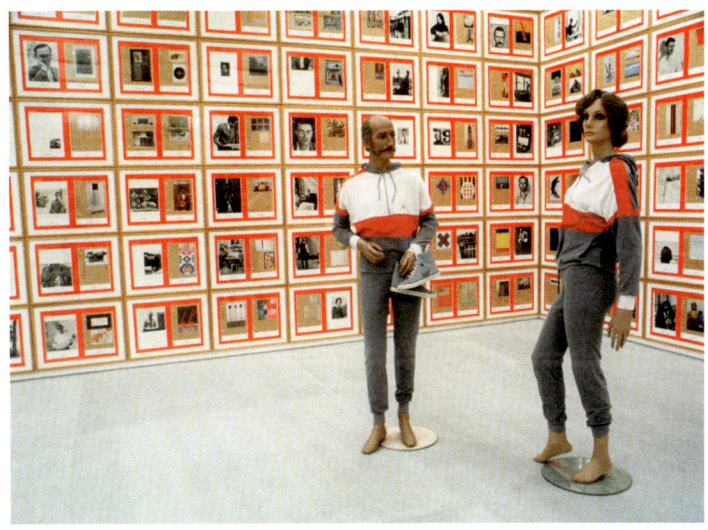

Josephine Meckseper, installation view, Kunstmuseum Stuttgart, 2007
Cultural History 1880–1983. Dia Center for the Arts, 1996–97

almost every doorway in New York. They are still available to be viewed online, at the New York Public Library.[17] During Darboven's years in New York, she clearly was exposed to the responses to the Vietnam War, namely the protests and antiwar marches in New York City. There are works—or details in her works—that directly relate to Vietnam and the protest against it.

There is an urgency to the way Darboven saw her responsibility as an artist living in postwar Germany. The way she recontextualizes the political climate of her time and salvages fragments of idealism stemming from the Enlightenment feels extremely relevant today. As art historian Dan Adler points out:

> For Darboven, the historian occupies the role of the "private" collector who must possess the materials he or she arranges and somehow make them his or her own. In *Cultural History*, ownership or the "thrill of being acquired" is indicated, for instance, by the photographs showing her sculptural objects, such as the mannequins, situated at her home. Benjamin identifies the private collector as one who resists the demands of capital; he or she renders the objects "useless" by orchestrating them into a new system or re-collection that exposes some "secret" historical meaning.[18]

Collecting and cataloguing an entire century, from Bismarck through Hitler to the Vietnam War, *Cultural History* encompasses extremely traumatic, irreconcilable events that the artist renders into one of the most important works of art of our time, by undoing, reperforming, and reframing them for us.

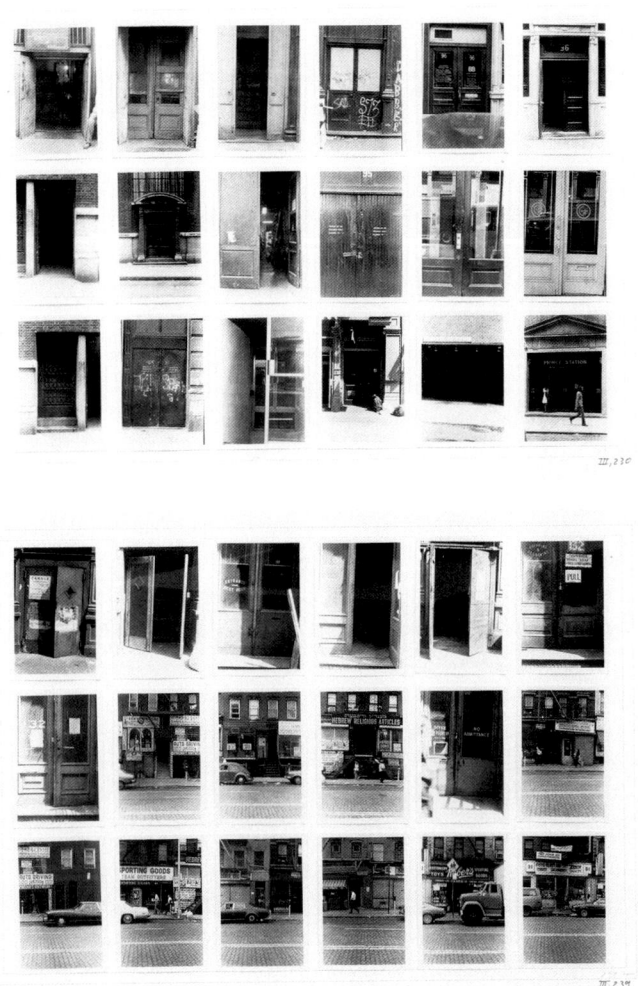

Cultural History 1880–1983. Detail: III/230
Cultural History 1880–1983. Detail: III/239

notes

1 In the brochure text that accompanied the 1996–97 exhibition, curator Lynne Cooke noted that *Cultural History 1880–1983* "resembles an encyclopedia rather than an archive; it feels exhaustive but, logically, cannot be. Like an encyclopedia, it catalogues and displays information without subordinating it to a dominant narrative form."

2 See Kira van Lil, "Introduction," in *Hanne Darboven: Menschen und Landschaften*, exh. cat. (Schaffhausen: Hallen für Neue Kunst, 1999), p. 10; and Rein Wolfs, "Hanne Darboven's Time Histories," in *Hanne Darboven: Zeitgeschichten—Enlightenment*, exh. cat. (Munich: Haus der Kunst, 2015), p. 19: "The inclusion of text passages from scholarly works that deal with Bismarck and his political morals illustrates the conscious historical contextualization in Darboven's artistic work."

3 "Nach Auschwitz ein Gedicht zu schreiben ist barbarisch." Theodor W. Adorno, "Kulturkritik und Gesellschaft" (1949), *Gesammelte Schriften*, vol. 10, p. 30. See Michael Newman, "Remembering and Repeating: Hanne Darboven's Work," *Robert Lehman Lectures on Contemporary Art*, no. 2 (New York: Dia Art Foundation, 2004), pp. 147, 154, n. 38.

4 *Architecture of Doom*, directed by Peter Cohen (Sweden, 1989; New York: First Run Features, 1991).

5 Newman, "Remembering and Repeating," pp. 144–46.

6 Verena Berger, *Hanne Darboven: Boundless* (Ostfildern: Hatje Cantz, 2015), p. 22.

7 "The Cabinet Papers 1915–1988," *National Archives* (UK), s.v. "Battle of Hamburg," http://www.nationalarchives.gov.uk/cabinetpapers/help/glossary-b.htm.

8 Hannah Arendt, *Eichmann in Jerusalem: A Report on the Banality of Evil* (New York: Viking, 1963), p. 115.

9 Roland Barthes, "Death of the Author," trans. Stephen Heath, in *Image-Music-Text* (New York: Macmillan, 1978), pp. 142–43.

10 Ibid., p. 145.

11 Theodor W. Adorno and Max Horkheimer, "Enlightenment as Mass Deception," in *Dialectic of Enlightenment* (1947; Stanford: Stanford University Press, 2002), pp. 94, 131.

12 Laura Emrick, "Interview with Dan Graham," *FAT 3* (1997), http://www.fatmagazine.us/3/graham.html.

13 *Cultural History* includes all of the issues of *Der Spiegel* from 1975 to 1979, a time capsule of events from the tragic late years of Germany's radical leftist movements. Newman, "Remembering and Repeating," p. 136.

14 Ulrike Meinhof, "Vom Protest zum Widerstand" ("From Protest to Resistance"), *Konkret 5* (May 1968), p. 5. See German History in Documents and Images, http://germanhistorydocs.ghi-dc.org/sub_document.cfm?document_id=895. Reprinted in *Everybody Talks about the Weather . . . We Don't: The Writings of Ulrike Meinhof*, ed. Karin Bauer (New York: Seven Stories Press, 2008), p. 242.

15 Excerpts are from the documentary "Baader Meinhof—In Love With Terror," *Generation Terror* (London: BBC, 2002).

16 Ulrike Meinhof, "Setting Fire to Department Stores" (1968), in *Everybody Talks about the Weather*, p. 246.

17 Roy Colmer, *Doors, NYC* (1976). New York Public Library Digital Collections, http://digitalcollections.nypl.org/collections/doors-nyc.

18 Dan Adler, *Hanne Darboven: Cultural History: 1880–1983* (London: Afterall, 2009), p. 54.

Josephine Meckseper's lecture on Hanne Darboven took place at Dia:Chelsea, New York, on April 4, 2011.

Matt Mullican
A Lecture on Hanne Darboven

I recently had this idea to use this opaque projector from my studio. It's a little noisy, but it's made for books, and I really do believe that that's at the core of what Hanne Darboven made: it's books; they are books. We see them on walls, but they're books, and of course we identify them as drawing, but she would argue the other.

This has been a remarkable time for me. Just going through her work and her psyche and meeting her and people who know a lot about her has been a fantastic experience. And a bit nerve-racking because I'm not an academic to presume to talk about another artist like this, someone whom I really don't know very well; it's a bit difficult. But my take on her work, in a funny sense, really does come out of this exhibition that I did at the Museum Ludwig in Cologne, *Learning from That Person's Work* (2005). It was remarkable to find certain similarities between my work and Darboven's work.

On October 19, 1973, Darboven wrote a letter to Sol LeWitt:

dear sol at hester street— / i do like to write / i don't like to read / this world is real / this word is frightening / this word is real / i don't like to read / i do like to write / all what is written I read / all what I write is written / i write / i don't describe / writing writing / there is nothing to describe / writing writing / i don't describe / i write / all what i write is written / all what is written i read / i do like to write / i don't like to read / this world is real / this world is frightening / this world is real / i don't like to read / i do like to write.[1]

One of the odd points is that if you turn this letter on its side, you'll see that it's absolutely symmetrical. In the center, above everything

October, 19, 1973, aullburgberg

dear sol at hesterstreet —
i do like to write
i don't like to read
this world is real
this word is frightening
this word is real
i don't like to read
i do like to write
all what is written i read
all what i write is written
i write
i d'out describe
writing writing
there is nothing to describe
writing writing
i d'out describe
i write
all what i write is written
all what is written i read
i do like to write
i d'out like to read
this world is real
this world is frightening
this world is real
i d'out like to read
i do like to write
———————— all ———————— 1

else, is "there is nothing to describe," and then, on either side of it, is "writing writing," "writing writing," "i don't describe," "i don't describe," "nothing to describe," up that way, except that this is "the word," and this is "the world," and it's a switch.

Hanne Darboven, born in 1941, graduated from the Hochschule für bildende Künste in Hamburg. In 1966–68 she sojourned to New York; she returned from there to Hamburg. I had a list of the titles of her exhibitions:

1967: *Constructions—Drawings*

1969: *Exhibition with 6 Film Projectors after 6 Books about 1968*

1970: *The Year 1970; Bulletin 28*

1971: *One Century in One Year*

1972: *Bulletin 64*

1974: *Drawings*; *El Lissitzky: Art and Pangeometry*; *One Month, One Year, One Century: Works from 1968 to 1974*; *24 Songs, A and B*

1975: *One Month, One Year, One Century: Works from 1968 to 1974*; *60 Works to 1 Work (60 Variants)*

1976: *Hanne Darboven: For Jean-Paul Sartre*

1977: *Milieu: Decampment in the Third Millennium*

1978: *J. J. Moser, The Law of Nations*

1979: *Bismarck Time*; *53 Weeks 1975*; *Drawings*

1980: *Milieu >80< –Today (for Walter Mehring)*; *Schreibzeit 75–80*, or in English, *Writing Time 75–80*

1981: *Turning Point >80<*

1982: *World Views*; *Turning Point >80<*

1983: *The Moon Has Risen*

1984: *Views >82<*

1987: *R. M. Rilke: The Book of Hours*; *Hanne Darboven: Bismarck Time*; *Hanne Darboven: Theatre*

1988: *Hanne Darboven: For Rainer Werner Fassbinder*; *Hanne Darboven: Editions 1978–88*

1989: *Existence*; *Requiem*; *Quartet >88<: Marie Curie, Rosa Luxemburg, Gertrude Stein, Virginia Woolf*

1990: *Hanne Darboven: Opus 26 Quartet Model 1–9, 1989/90*; *Hanne Darboven: For Abraham Lincoln*; *Hanne Darboven: Kurt Schwitters*; *Hanne Darboven: Primitive Time/Clock Time*

1991: *Evolution >86<*; *The Winged Earth: Requiem*

1992: *Works 1971, 1974, 1983, 1987, 1990*

1993: *Cruise to Hell*

1994: *Homage to My Father*; *Homage to My Mother*

1995: *South Korean Calendar, 1991*; *Four Books*

1996: *Milieu >80< – Today (for Walter Mehring)*; *Evolution Leibniz, 1986*; *Debit and Credit*; *Cultural History 1880–1983*

1997: *Children of This World*

1998: *Stone of Wisdom 1996*

1999: First publication of *Writing Time*; *Homage to Picasso*; *The Early Work*; *My Childhood, My School Days, My Academy Days*; *Living A I, II*; *B I, II*; *C I, II*; *D I, II*

2000: *People and Landscapes*

2002: *The Books 1966–2002*; *Cosmos >85< –Journey Around the World–In Memory of Humboldt–Cosmos*[2]

And *One Century ABC* in 2004 is the most recent entry on my list.

And here is a list of people that she has used as subject matter within her work: Charles Baudelaire, Heinrich Heine, Karl Cross, Otto von Bismarck, Bertolt Brecht, Rainer Werner Fassbinder, Jean-Paul Sartre, Friedrich II, Johann Wolfgang von Goethe, El Lissitzky, Albrecht Dürer, Abraham Lincoln, Gottfried Wilhelm Leibniz, Homero Manzi, Celedonio Flores, Rainer Maria Rilke, Lord Ernest Rutherford, Niels Bohr, Marie Curie, Rosa Luxemburg, Gertrude Stein, Virginia Woolf, Pablo Picasso, Eugen Herrigel, and Georg Christoph Lichtenberg.

I've read so many magazine articles on Darboven that I became interested in the way people defined her through their titles. "Time and Time Again," that's one; "Marking Time," that's another; "Hanne Darboven, or the Dimensions of Time and Culture," that's another; "Today Crossed Out"; "Hanne Darboven: Deep in Numbers"; "On a Number of Things"; "The Numbers Game"; "Work Ennobles—I'm Staying Bourgeois"; "System as Desire: Hanne Darboven"; "*Schreibzeit*"; "Hanne Darboven's Time: The Content of Consciousness"; "*Primitive Time/Clock Time*"; "*Darboven: The Sculpting of Time*"; "My Work Ends in Music: Hanne Darboven's Notations as Musical Works."[3]

Artists that have been mentioned in relation to her: Sol LeWitt, Donald Judd, Carl Andre, John Cage, Karlheinz Stockhausen, On Kawara, Robert Morris, Jenny Holzer, Barbara Kruger, Adolf Wölfli, Ad Reinhardt, Lawrence Weiner, and Eva Hesse.

Now, we're kind of doing a little bit of what her letter did. I am going to be reading some quotes from these various articles and I'll just leave a little space around each one.[4]

"My invention, mathematical prose."

"Real writing."

Spatial models:

"Fantasy assembled out of numbers, angles, lines, points, planes, spaces, to create an environment that would contain variety and create a whole. I'm very happy to have made it and to see it now. It's a discovery for me, stimulating, beautiful, yes. Labyrinthine, labile, strange."

"Numbers are the most neutral way of talking about things. No names, no objects, just the counting of numbers and the use of dates."

Objects:

"So-called art has become its own value, it's a product by which I mean a product of contemplation and action. Virtuosity and originality are its message. In fact this art has become highly subjective. One is no longer bound to anything, one has nothing on behalf of which to convey a message. Art no longer mediates as once. For example, history painting did a change for the better, or perhaps not. Yes, I suppose, a change for the better. Autonomy has been one, as it was earlier in music and literature. I see I'm beginning to talk shop. Enough of that."

Message:

"My work surely isn't incomprehensible, manipulation of data in the sense of our computer age."

"One is one is one. *Ein ist eins ist eins.*"

"Every woman."

"Flowers wither."

"Dear Papa, I am taking this opportunity to send you some more bills, realities, so sad and also not, facts, realities, values to which, in our contemporary world of worthless objects, one must indeed attach a certain value. They are after all the only supports, realities."

Her work:

"Scrap paper economy to keep on administering. At the moment, I am working cheaply with *The New York Times* as my material. Made two *collages* out of the stock exchange pages. One of the *collages* is really quite beautiful. The numbers, printed so densely, they almost appear as stripes, completely monochrome + monotone. Much could be done with this. In fact, it has often been remarked that my numbers have something of this materiality, the stock exchange. Past time revived."

Today:

"Because they are so steady, limited, artificial, the only thing that has ever been created is the number. I write and don't describe and I do like to write and don't like to read. Daily writing."

Old world:

"I build up something by having disturbed something. Destruction becomes construction. Action interrupts contemplation as the means of accepting something among many given alternatives, for accepting nothing becomes chaos. A system became necessary. How else could I in a concentrated way find something of interest which lends itself to continuation? My systems are numerical concepts which work in terms of progressions and/or reductions akin to musical themes with variations."

"Because 'No more words' is a writing process, it's not a drawing process. The writing fills the space as a drawing would. It turns out to be aesthetic, but that wasn't my first aim."

Daily numbers:

"Writing is the dimension of consciousness. Our work is not a philosophy nor a science of the physical world. It is itself an element of the physical world and can as such only be an object of science."

"Novel."

"Individual mythology."

"All one piece."

"Brain waves."

"Fiction."

"My novel. A real book."

"There are no aesthetic tricks, it is that way, no search, no research, just writing, but the complete thing must be done before the typing begins."

"So I learned where I came from by doing it. It becomes not more and more because it's already there, but clearer and clearer."

"Read. Look at. Mathematics. Nothing. I choose numbers because they are so steady, limited, artificial. The only thing that's ever been created is the number, a number of something. Two chairs or whatever is something else, it's not numbers and has other meanings. If I were making it up, I couldn't possibly write all that. It has to be totally simple to be real writing. Still, each time I have to write it becomes so calm, and so normal, there is no story, there's nothing to figure out, not a secret, but still exciting. I feel myself not thinking what other people think, but what I think. I write for myself, there is no other way. This is for me, going on, it's an enormous thing to do."

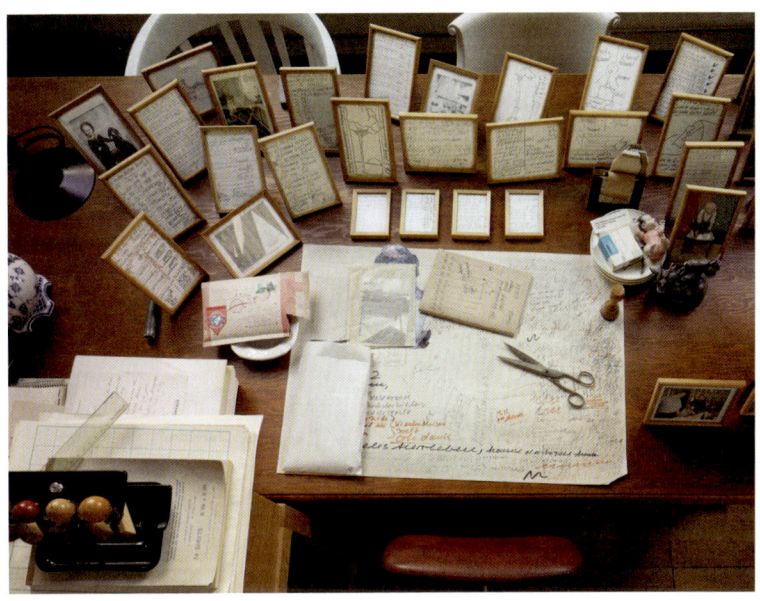

Writing desk, Garret, Am Burgberg, Hamburg-Rönneburg, 2013

Her writing becomes her drawing. Her writing is beautiful. The act of writing uses a different part of the brain than the act of drawing. Does the act of copying use a different part of the brain than the act of creating? One of the things that I realized in the trance state,[5] and that's where I'm heading, is that the person or the character that I am dealing with in the trance state loves to copy. It's his favorite thing to do, this mindless act of just copying text. He has copied restaurant menus and he has copied labels from cereal boxes and coffee containers. And realizing that he is free when he copies. He's absolutely free.

What does the math represent? What does the chart represent? Another thing that happens in the trance state is numbers. The first subject that I ever wrote in the trance state—this was in the 1970s—was numbers. The trance state, when you go into a trance state you are counting backward, and as you count backward you are going deeper and deeper and deeper . . . and at the end you are in a pretty deep trance and thus what happens is that numbers themselves act as a kind of a point of pattern.

Meaning without words. What meaning? Meaning behind the words, under the words, before the words, after the words. Do we think in words or do we think in pictures? I don't think it's either one. I think we think in patterns and sequences of evolving contexts. We feel our place within those contexts, and doing so defines our place within them, thus orienting ourselves to their possible outcome or multiple outcomes. The meaning is thus primarily emotional, as that defines our relationship to the context.

Patterns of behavior: I myself believe that I live in this world in a mindless kind of trance. I go through the motions of walking, changing, driving, cooking, talking, et cetera; the pattern of behavior has an implication and/or consequence which I feel and according to which I act.

When I met Darboven, I was driven out to her house. A meeting had been set up a month or two beforehand.[6] She lived in the same house that her parents had lived in, and it's an amazing place to visit. And we were to have lunch at this Italian restaurant, and I think she had been going to that same Italian restaurant for twenty-five years. When I went there to her house, she said, "Please walk through the house." Then I came back after walking through the house. She said, "Sit down for forty-five minutes," and she turned on the record player and played me a piece of music. Then we got to the restaurant; finally she sat down. And when she entered the restaurant it was kind of incredible. Because this is a wonderful restaurant, and this was on a Sunday, because that's the day, I think, that she had visitors. But the entire staff was at attention, and they escorted her to our table and sat her down, and they knew exactly what she wanted to drink and to eat, and she had one glass, and that was it. And I had one thing to say. I was talking about this issue of meaning and thought, and the fact that in thinking about the idea of thinking, do we think in words? And I said, I don't think I think in words. Do we think in pictures? I don't think we think in pictures. I think we think in an evolving context and also the brain does not work in a linear fashion. I think we think on many levels at once. When I walk and talk and drive a car and am dealing with my kids in the backseat, it's all happening at once, and I am easily designating all of that information. And I told her that I think that what we're thinking is closer to music than it is to symbols. Visually, I thought her work and the way that it functions somehow seems to emulate this abstraction, what's behind the picture. When I say "I want," I'm working out something. It's changing from one moment to the next. As I said, my orientation to it is shifting and the consequences move. And that is very similar to the way you can see her work or as you enter her work.

This thought, I feel, is a base element in Darboven's work. She placed patterns on a page, evolving patterns that we can enter and exit at will, given our understanding of her context and content. I sense that what she aimed to do was to mark or define thought in the abstract, without words, without pictures. But pictures do enter her work in the form of photos, postcards, magazines, science, et cetera. I have not found an explanation from her as to how they function—for instance, the relationship of the postcards to her numerical systems. Perhaps they act as markers for a time or a place. Similar to a scrapbook, defining the life of its maker, then becoming anchors or symbols for that given context or pattern.

The act of marking time is a very basic act. As in the man in prison marking the days he has spent there and thinking about the days that he has yet to spend there. It's that first 1, 2, 3, 4, 5, 1, 2, 3, 4, 5, 1, 2, 3, 4, 5. . . . The calendar, the diary, the appointment book that you may have, could be considered a creative act; but beyond the practical use of objectifying your time, or your use of time, a kind of extension of memory, why do it? Why collect? Why compute? For whose benefit? I've collected collections of sugar packets, matchbox covers, scrapbooks, photo albums . . . all of which took years for their makers to complete and at the end were sold for very little money or even given away. What does it mean to write down my thoughts of a time and a place that within years will have no consequence to my or any other lives?

This impulse to document our lives is very basic, strong, and human . . . a very basic and strong response to the human condition. We put ourselves into the book as if to extend our lives within its pages. This could also be said for the collecting of objects. They, as well, mark time and represent contexts long gone, like souvenirs from trips taken to exotic places. Not only do they evoke those places, but

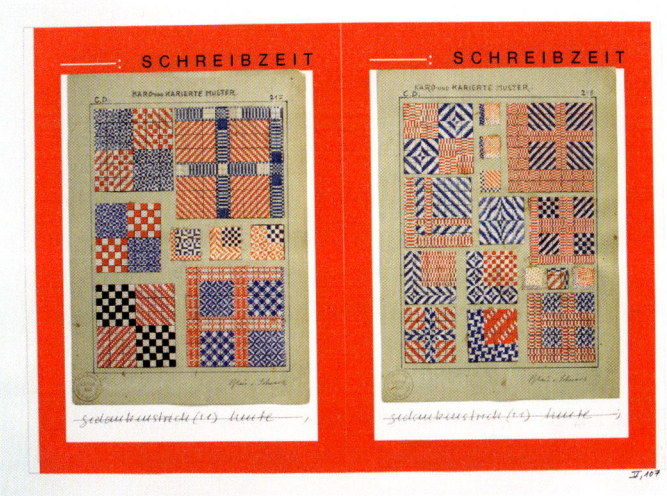

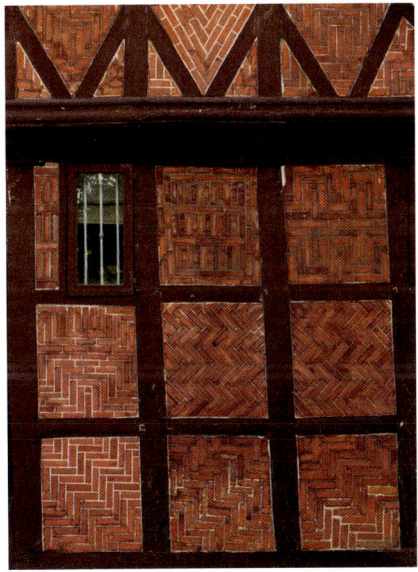

Cultural History 1880–1983, 1980–83. Detail: V/107
Barn, Am Burgberg, 2013

represent our feelings and our relationship to those places. They're something like monuments.

If the patterns pointing to music represent the thought prior to a kind of meaning, the photos, the objects, may represent that to which we respond to meaningfully, the whole project being a self-contained world. This is not the case when viewing Darboven's work. She was an extremely ambitious artist, working with huge contexts, as I have said earlier—the twentieth century as a single work. The complex literary markings of centuries, with persons like Otto von Bismarck, Marie Curie, Pablo Picasso, and Jean-Paul Sartre, marking their influences.

Notating. Energy in the effort of marking time.

Entering a Darboven exhibit, the first thought is work and—this is absolutely crucial—time. But not in the sense of time represented as in a calendar, but in time spent. The subject of the process is held in balance with the time represented. The subject of mathematics, the subject of history, the subject of philosophy, the subject of writing, and the exercise of writing. Hand in hand with that, you have the photo album, the scrapbook, the postcard, the diary—you have this, in a sense, very learned, scholarly representation of the object and of the writing, and this almost basic, fundamental something that everybody does.

To cover a wall, a space, with any book page, framed in a sequence; that means to cover a wall with a book. If I get this catalogue and I just put it all up on the wall, it doesn't matter where, this brings to mind Darboven. This is taking the act, this is taking something that has to be read in time and representing it spatially. It's again very basic. Abstracting meaning in time into meaning in space. This could be similar to the marking down of experience, objectifying the subjective all within a singularly accurate mechanical system.

I saw an exhibition of Darboven's books in Vienna.[7] It was two floors and it was endless, it just did not stop. There were just cases upon cases upon cases upon . . . it was nuts. It was insane but beautiful, one of the most beautiful exhibitions I have ever seen. And I just wanted to show you somehow the way these things may function when they are not on the wall, because we're much more familiar, say, with how these things function in space. And when you cover a wall with these pictures, it brings to mind an unfathomable context. How does one make sense? How do you orient yourself? You can try and start, to work yourself through it. I am interested in the experience of being outside and seeing the amount of energy that goes into this. Also, the fact that everything is somehow in relationship to everything else and it's all purposeful, there are no accidents here. It all makes for this abstract point. And it's kind of boggling, tremendous—tremendous. One of the things that I wanted to do, was to actually work out one of Darboven's systems. It is a huge task to participate in the content of a work—not the visual aspect of a work, but what it represents and what it means and how the whole thing evolves. I was talking with several people who really know her work very, very well, and one of the things I wanted to do would be to work out one drawing from beginning to end so we can basically understand it, so we can follow that chain of events. And I would pick a drawing and the person who really knows their stuff would start and then at one point they'd give up. And then they would have to go back into it, and they know their stuff, so we'd get through it. It's a struggle, but that's part of the subject, that has to do with it.

Also, one thinks of her in her house, and her house is incredible. As she said, before she types it's all worked out already, so there's a lot of time when she's not writing, there has to be. Or is it a kind of automatic writing where she would somehow create all of the systems, the cross-references, the whole algorithm, and how it evolves? Or does it just come to her? I don't think so. I think she had to work it all out before she began the process of writing out those 45,000 pages. And the method of how she did it, when and how she worked, it was the regimentality of her life.

So now I'm going to try and work out one page. Here is one page of Darboven's work *00–99 / 100 à 19 x 42 No. / 2K–61K* (1970).

This is a century. There you see a little *K* behind each number—there's a *K*, there's 2K, 3K, 4K, 5K, and it goes all the way up to 61K. And these are K numbers, or K-values. Now, the numbers themselves are the addition of a day, a month, and a year. My birthday is September 18, 1951, and what I would do would be to add 18 for the day, 9 for the month, 5 and then 1, not 51, but 5 and then 1, and I get 33. That's my number. And you'll find it there, there it is, there I am, that's my birthday, that's my number.

Within this triangle the most frequent numbers in the century are in the middle; and the least frequent are at top and bottom; there's only one double zero and there's only one number 2 and there's only one number 61. And 61 would be the last day of December 1999, that would be 61K, and there's only one.

There are forty-two variations for each year in this triangle, and we're going to work our way across. In the first one, it would be January 1st, so January is 1 and then the 1st is 1 and then 00 so that's the 2K, and that happens once. That means in that yearlong period, the highest number that you could have is 43, that's the highest number, if you added up all the points. Between 2K and 43K there are forty-two possible sums. And then if you go down to another year, for instance, to 99, the highest number is 61K, and there is only one of those. So these are all the different years, and you'll see that they are duplicates, and triplicates, and so forth.

It's kind of a remarkable system. Everything has this K number. This is a century, and Darboven could have this among thousands of other pages that would work out this endless, refined change of these

½—19/ Index: 00 — 99 / 100' à 19× 42 No | 2K— 61K

2 K — 61 K

1.	2 K —43K—1 X —00,			42 No
2.	3 K —44K—2 X —01, 10,			42 No
3.	4 K —45K—3 X —02, 11, 20,			42 No
4.	5 K —46K—4 X —03, 12, 21, 30,			42 No
5.	6 K —47K—5 X —04, 13, 22, 31, 40,			42 No
6.	7 K —48K—6 X —05, 14, 23, 32, 41, 50,			42 No
7.	8 K —49K—7 X —06, 15, 24, 33, 42, 51, 60,			42 No
8.	9 K —50K—8 X —07, 16, 25, 34, 43, 52, 61, 70,			42 No
9.	10 K —51K—9 X —08, 17, 26, 35, 44, 53, 62, 71, 80,			42 No
10.	11 K —52K—10X—09, 18, 27, 36, 45, 54, 63, 72, 81, 90,			42 No
11.	12 K —53K—9 X —19, 28, 37, 46, 55, 64, 73, 82, 91,			42 No
12.	13 K —54K—8 X —29, 38, 47, 56, 65, 74, 83, 92,			42 No
13.	14 K —55K—7 X —39, 48, 57, 66, 75, 84, 93,			42 No
14.	15 K —56K—6 X —49, 58, 67, 76, 85, 94,			42 No
15.	16 K —57K—5 X —59, 68, 77, 86, 95,			42 No
16.	17 K —58K—4 X —69, 78, 87, 96,			42 No
17.	18 K —59 K—3X—79, 88, 97,			42 No
18.	19 K —60K—2 X —89, 98,			42 No
19.	20K —61K—1 X —99,			42 No

2 K — 61 K   hanne darboven, 1970 —

sequences. It's the calendar. And the calendar is such a basic concept . . . as I mentioned earlier with the prisoner and the marking of the days.

And then there is the index, 00 to 99, and then there's a slash and 100, 19 x 42, 2K to 61K. I'm not certain, but the K-value represents a construction, and, she deals in centuries. That's another point, so you get some idea of how these things progress. It almost makes that time spatial in how it's represented. It's like an architecture of sorts.

Some things refer in a really basic way to Darboven's work but are not her work.

I've been collecting, as I said, scrapbooks, postcard collections, photo albums, all kinds of stuff. Darboven seemed to represent something that is so complex and so academic and high, and yet here this is also what she is doing, and she was making comments by using them, having to do with this need to simply fill this book, to have this in proximity.

Another point of reference for Darboven was her father, and the life of the businessman and the daily grind. At least in the actions of what she did. The addition, the caring over, the constant . . . this working without working. This representation of work. This representation of the daily life of quite a few people. And in relationship to numbers. It's quite something.

Here is a facsimile page from Denis Diderot's *Encyclopédie* on the art of writing. This point of reference is about penmanship. It's about getting the drawing of the line in a way . . . it's an exercise to write in a more fluid and aesthetic manner. It's something I've been very attracted to. And I just wanted to show that in the context of the loopy stuff, Darboven's cursive writing.

This connects to my work with hypnosis. For example, for a countdown from 99 to 1, I say the word "relax" behind each number. The point is that that is a really great way to make yourself relaxed. Because the number itself gets it deeper. Somehow when you repeat the

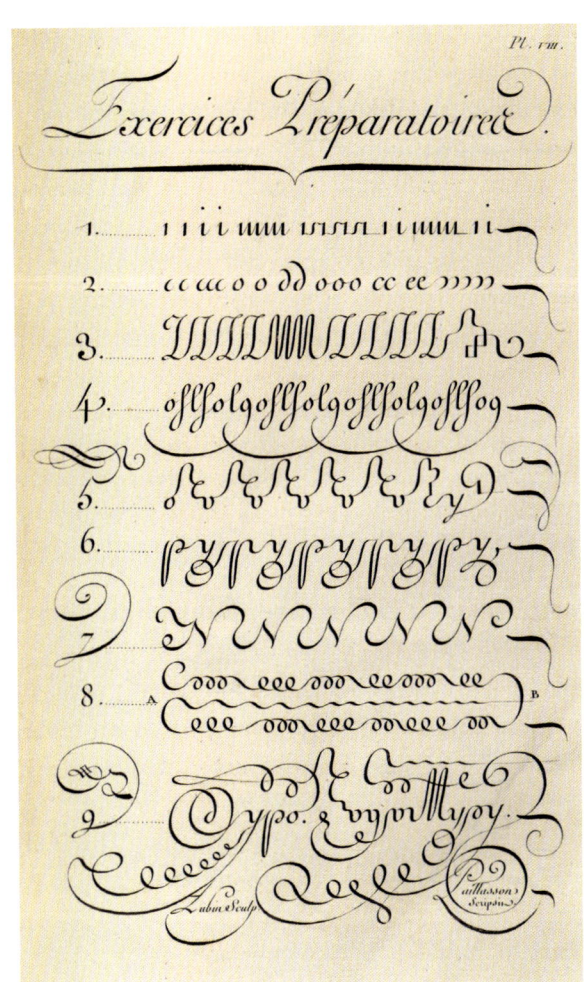

"Exercices Préparatoire," from *Encyclopédie*, 1751–72

number, it goes deeper into your consciousness. The abstraction of the number is very important in terms of getting you deeper. And then here it's just numbers going down on the side of the paper.

The reason I mention this has to do with the relationship of the psyche to the numbers, and I was very aware after I did this, that it was like some marking of time very similar to that of Darboven . . . this "I" that she repeats again and again and again and again.

Now I am going to read the second half. This is a letter to Sol LeWitt, October 6.

> Dear Sol. And what an irony. I choose liberal writing. I choose number, "date," numbers, liberal writing—not to be used—and vice versa it developed and even I have to use dates. Now by using them—ironical— but as I wrote to you, Sol: season follows season, creates it, call it, it, and I do hope we'll return to it—I will—writing, liberal writing, writing as quiet as pencil and paper, as writing is writing, this is my field, points to it, this is my limit, points to it, this is my desire, points to it. And I will work for this, points to it. And I will work this for, points to it. For writing,—writing—it, call it, it. Dear Sol, page 4.[8]

In 1968 Darboven did a series of film animation pieces (*Sechs Bücher über 1968* [*Six Books about 1968*]). The thing is that I felt that somehow, as I said, to work out that single drawing, and to kind of get a sense of how she functions . . . this is an impossible task, to figure this out. But you see, there it is, 14K, 14K, it's a growing point. This is like a twenty-minute film. But it kind of takes the pressure off me to try and actually figure out the piece.

It is refusing my will. It's not accommodating any. . . . You can't do it. Because there is not enough time to do it, it's impossible. So then does it become decorative, at that point? Or does it simply become something that really is going to happen with or without you and you can see it as best as you can but you're not going to get it?

She gives you so much stuff to work with in terms of history and everything else, and at the same time she's keeping you at bay.

Oct. 6, 1973, amy burg berg
dear undn dear sol
and what am i romy —
i choose liberal writing —
i choose number- "date"- numm.
bers — liberal writing —
not be used —
and vice verse it developed
and even i have to use dates
now by using them —
       i r o n i c a l —
but as i wrote to you, SOL:
reason follows reason/creates ";A"
Call "iA" "A"
and i do hope/will, return
to ";A" dash i will dash
writing liberal writing —
writing as quiet as pencil and
paper as writing is writing —
this is my field → "iA"
this is my limit → "iA"
this is my desire → "iA"
and i will work for this→"iA"
and i will work this for→ "iA"
for writing-writing —
        "iA"
call "it" "A" / dear sol
        page ④

Letter from Hanne Darboven to Sol LeWitt, 1973

125

Certainly. She's keeping you away. She does the work for herself, that's absolutely clear. Because I think she's the only one that could understand this film. Maybe people, scholars. . . . There's 24K, 24K. . . . And I bet you that this refers to the amount of time that that screen is lit, and/or the black screen. That those numbers are referenced to the time, in milliseconds or seconds, in relationship to the making of this movie, perhaps the frames of film. And it doesn't stop at the bottom, it keeps going and going and going. And I think the sequences change as well. Okay, let's return to the house.

The Statue of Liberty is outside the house. It's like a little bit of America. This is the most eccentric person I've ever met in my entire life. She's an extraordinary individual.

There is a table where she used to sit. It's right in front of a sink. The sink no longer works, but she would sit in front of it.

This was a drawing table. This was where she worked, and now it's a monument. We have all the objects from that period. She might have worked there in the 1970s.

She had a small closet that was devoted to her mother. And she, for many, many, many years, had goats—Micky, Mama Micky, and Kleine Micky. They're in the back, they have their own shed in the other part of the house. They've always been named Micky, and as they died, she had them stuffed, and they become part of this house. And yet they all have . . . there are graves, there's a cemetery in the back where they are all properly buried as well. So their images become part of the house itself.

Another point of the house is that this is public, where we may go is a public part of the house, maybe her studio that is active, and her bedroom no one goes into, that is private. And so, her house, which is 95 percent public now, I mean public in the sense that I was allowed to walk there. No one can just come in, you have to be introduced and she has to have the time.

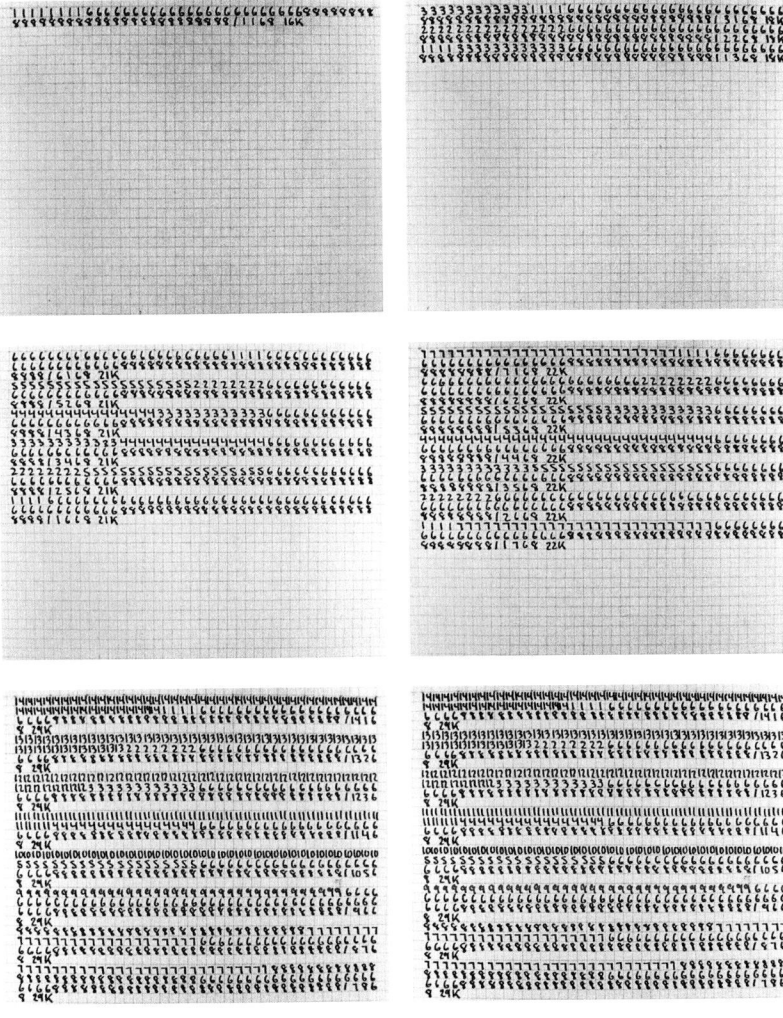

Sechs Bücher über 1968 (Six Books about 1968), 1968   127

And the house itself is no longer a house. It's changed.[9] She would hang out in the kitchen because that was where the refrigerator was. And she could put her drinks in there and sit there. But then she didn't drink anymore, but she would sit there.[10]

I'm interested in this whole issue of how . . . in the role of the objects in relationship to the role of the math, and of the sequence, the patterning. The two are so extreme. She's an incredibly ambitious person. Nothing is halfway.

She's had an exhibition at the Deutsche Guggenheim in Berlin, *Hommage à Picasso*.[11] As part of it, there was a musical work. When I visited there, as I said, she sat me down, and for forty-five minutes I heard this piece. It all follows the system, these numbers, these K numbers. The K numbers are referring to the different notes, and the different bars, and the whole thing, it's all done. And you can hear, at the end of each section, a kind of a "prrrip," and that is, I think that's the year or the day or the sequence, the end of the sequence, where all the numbers gather again and they have this kind of counting thing.

And now I'd like to end with her music, because it's too good.

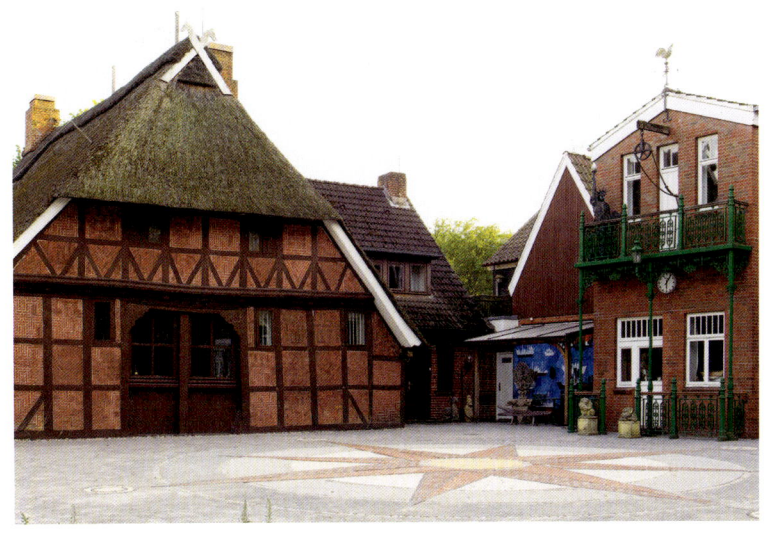

Am Burgberg, 2013

notes

1 Hanne Darboven to Sol LeWitt, October 19, 1973.

2 Though listed in English, the majority of the exhibitions listed here were originally German-language titles.

3 The following articles are being referenced: Mark Gisbourne, "Time and Time Again: Interview with Hanne Darboven," *Art Monthly*, no. 181 (November 1994), pp. 3–6; Isabelle Graw, "Marking Time and Writing in the Work of Hanne Darboven," *Artscribe International*, no. 79 (January/February 1990), pp. 68–71; Jean-Pierre Bordaz, "Hanne Darboven, or the Dimension of Time and Culture," *Parkett*, no. 10 (September 1986), pp. 104–11; Coosje van Bruggen, "Today Crossed Out, an Introduction by Coosje van Bruggen to *Today*, a Project by Hanne Darboven," *Artforum* 26, no. 5 (January 1988), pp. 70–73; Lucy Lippard, "Hanne Darboven: Deep in Numbers," *Artforum* 12, no. 2 (October 1973), pp. 35–39; Dorothea Dietrich, "On a Number of Things," *On Paper* 2, no. 1 (Fall 1997), pp. 15–19; John Anthony Thwaites, "The Numbers Game," *Art and Artists* 6, no. 10 (January 1972), pp. 24–25; Isabelle Graw, "Work Ennobles—I'm Staying Bourgeois," in *Inside the Visible: An Elliptical Traverse of 20th Century Art in, of, and from the Feminine*, ed. Catherine de Zegher (Cambridge, Mass.: MIT Press, 1996), pp. 246–55; Donald Kuspit, "System as Desire: Hanne Darboven," *Art in America* 68, no. 6 (Summer 1980), pp. 118–19; Berhard Jussen, ed., *Hanne Darboven. Schreibzeit* (Göttingen: Max-Planck-Institut für Geschichte; Cologne: Walther König, 2000); Annelie Pohlen, "Hanne Darboven's Time: The Content of Consciousness," *Artforum* 21, no. 8 (April 1983), pp. 52–53; *Hanne Darboven: Primitive Zeit/ Uhrzeit = Primitive Time/Clock Time*, exh. cat. Goldie Paley Gallery, Moore College of Art and Design (Philadelphia: The Gallery, 1990); Ingrid Burgbacher-Krupka, *Hanne Darboven. Konstruiert, literarisch, musikalisch/Constructed, Literary, Musical: The Sculpting of Time*, exh. cat. Goethe-Institute, London (Ostfildern-Ruit: Cantz, 1994); and Sibylle Omlin, "My Work Ends in Music: Hanne Darboven's Notations as Musical Works," *Parkett*, no. 67 (2003), pp. 126–29.

4 The citations are from the following sources: Hanne Darboven, "Artists on Their Art," *Art International* 12, no. 4 (April 20, 1968), p. 55; Lippard,

"Hanne Darboven: Deep in Numbers," pp. 35–39; Bordaz, "Hanne Darboven, or the Dimension of Time and Culture," pp. 104–11; van Bruggen, "Today Crossed Out," pp. 70–73; Gisbourne, "Time and Time Again," pp. 3–6; *Hanne Darboven: Menschen und Landschaften*, exh. cat. Hallen für neue Kunst, Schaffhausen (Hamburg: Christians-Verlag, 1999), particularly the essay by Brigid Doherty, "Hanne Darboven: 'Real Writing' of History," pp. 31–47.

5 Matt Mullican has been experimenting with trance states since 1977.

6 The meeting was arranged through the kind intervention of Susanne Liebelt.

7 *Hanne Darboven: Bücher*, Museum Moderner Kunst Stiftung Ludwig, Vienna, September 20–November 23, 2003.

8 Hanne Darboven to Sol LeWitt, October 6, 1973.

9 The house and the kitchen have been transformed into a living archive of her art and life.

10 As she sat in the kitchen by the refrigerator, she put a record on the turntable and played a piece of her music.

11 *Hanne Darboven: Hommage à Picasso*, Deutsche Guggenheim, Berlin, February 4–April 23, 2006. Opus 60 was performed by the Junge Sinfonie Berlin in 2006, conducted by Aurélien Bello.

Matt Mullican's lecture on Hanne Darboven took place at Dia:Chelsea, New York, on March 13, 2006.

CONTRIBUTORS

Gregg Bordowitz is an artist and a writer. His lecture-performance *Sex Mitigating Death: On Discourse and Drives: A Meditative Poem* was presented at the Tate Modern in London in 2011. His films, including *Fast Trip, Long Drop* (1993), *The Suicide* (1996), and *Habit* (2001), have been screened internationally. His most recent book, *General Idea: Imagevirus*, was published by Afterall in 2010. His book of poetry, *Volition*, was published by Printed Matter in 2009, and a collection of his writings, *The AIDS Crisis Is Ridiculous and Other Writings 1986–2003*, was published by MIT Press in 2004. He is currently the director of the Low-Residency MFA program at the School of the Art Institute of Chicago.

Sam Lewitt was born in Los Angeles in 1981. His recent solo exhibitions include *Less Light Warm Words* at the Swiss Institute for Contemporary Art, New York (2016), *More Heat Than Light* at Kunsthalle Basel (2016) and the CCA Wattis Institute for Contemporary Art, San Francisco (2015), *Verbrannte Erde: Second Salvage* at the Leopold Hoesch Museum, Düren, Germany (2014), and *International Corrosion Fatigue* at Galerie Buchholz, Cologne (2013). His work was also included in the Whitney Biennial, New York, in 2012. Lewitt lives and works in New York.

Josephine Meckseper was born in Lilienthal, Germany, in 1964. Her recent solo exhibitions include presentations at Neuer Aachener Kunstverein, Aachen, Germany (2014), the Parrish Art Museum, Water Mill, New York (2013), Migros Museum für Gegenwartskunst, Zurich (2009), and Museum of Modern Art, New York (2008). In 2015 her works were included in *America Is Hard to See* at the Whitney Museum of Art, New York, and *Storylines* at the Solomon R. Guggenheim Museum, New York. Meckseper lives and works in New York.

Matt Mullican was born in Santa Monica in 1951. He has had solo museum exhibitions at the Museum of Modern Art, New York (1989), Museu Serralves, Porto, Portugal (2000), Kunsthalle, Basel (2001), Museum Ludwig, Cologne (2005), and Lentos Kunstmuseum, Linz (2006), among other international venues. His work was also included in the Whitney Biennial, New York, in 2008. Mullican lives and works in New York and Berlin.

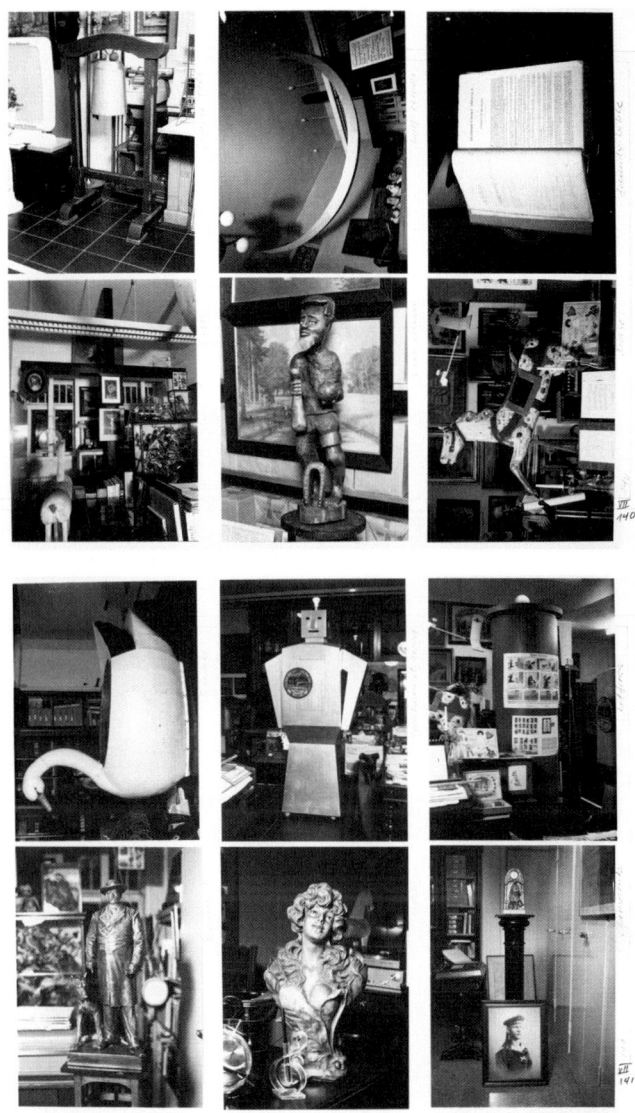

Cultural History 1880–1983. Detail: VII/140
Cultural History 1880–1983. Detail: VII/141

PHOTO CREDITS

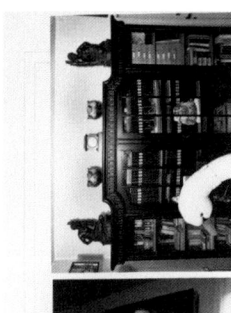
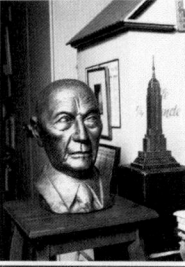
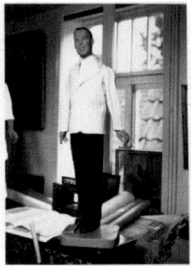
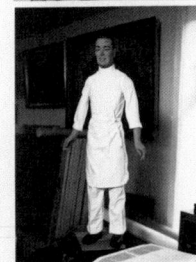
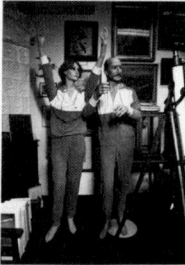
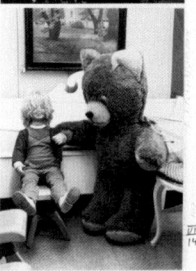
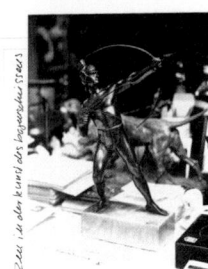

Cultural History 1880−1983. Detail: VII/142
Cultural History 1880−1983. Detail: VII/143